Colonel
ANDREW COWAN

Colonel ANDREW COWAN

Union Soldier, Louisville Citizen, Peacemaker

BRYAN S. BUSH

Acclaim Press
MORLEY, MISSOURI

Acclaim Press
— Your Next Great Book —

P.O. Box 238
Morley, MO 63767
(573) 472-9800
www.acclaimpress.com

Book Design: Devon Burroughs
Cover Design: M. Frene Melton

Library of Congress Control Number: 2014920254
ISBN-13: 978-1-938905-86-5
ISBN-10: 1-938905-86-5

First Printing: 2015
Printed in the United States of America
10 9 8 7 6 5 4 3 2 1

Cover photos:

Andrew Cowan. Courtesy of the Library of Congress

Central Park, Louisville, Ky., ca. 1900-1910. Photo by Detroit Publishing Co. Courtesy of the Library of Congress.

Medals courtesy of author's personal collection.

Burside Bridge, Battle of Antietam. Courtesy of the Library of Congress.

Bridge #5 at Cherokee Park, Louisville, Ky, ca. 1921. Photo by Caufield and Shook, Louisville, Ky. Courtesy of the Library of Congress.

Iroquois Park, observation point on top of hill, looking toward Louisville, ca. 1922. Photo by Caufield and Shook, Louisville, Ky. Courtesy of the Library of Congress.

CONTENTS

Introduction

In 1848, Andrew Cowan sailed with his family to America from Ayrshire, Scotland and arrived in New York. His family hoped that young Andrew Cowan would live the American dream and become successful at his new life in America. Cowan studied in school and entered Madison University, now Colgate University. When the Civil War broke out in April of 1861, President Abraham Lincoln called for seventy-five thousand volunteers. Cowan quit the University and heeded President Lincoln's call for soldiers. At the young age of twenty, he joined the Union army and enlisted in the New York regiment and later the 1st New York Independent Battery.

During the Civil War, he fought in several Eastern Theater battles, including the Battle of Williamsburg, the Peninsular Campaign, Fredericksburg, Antietam, Chancellorsville, Gettysburg, the Mine Run Campaign, the Rapidan and James River Campaign, the Shenandoah Valley Campaign, Battle of the Wilderness, Spotsylvania, Cold Harbor, the siege and fall of Petersburg, the repulse of Confederate General Jubal Early's attack on Washington, D.C., Sailor's Creek, and the surrender at Appomattox. During the Civil War, he was severely wounded at Gilbert's Ford, on September 13, 1864, but returned to duty a month later on October 23. On December 21, 1864, he was appointed chief of artillery of the 6th Corps. He was especially known for his actions at Gettysburg during Confederate General George Pickett's charge, where he defended the "Bloody Angle."

After the War, he was widely known as the father of the joint reunion of the blue and gray at Gettysburg on the fiftieth anniversary of the Battle of Gettysburg. He headed the firm of Andrew Cowan & Company, established in 1866, as a wholesale hardware, leather, and mill supply store in Louisville. He became a very successful businessman and became president of the National Oak Leather Company, director of the National Bank of Commerce, Fidelity, and Columbia Trust Company.

During 1883 to 1887, he was on the board of directors for the Southern Exposition. The Southern Exposition was a very early version of the World's Fair, and showcased industrial and agricultural products from the North and South, but also showcased pavilions from all over the world, including Japan, Mexico, Sweden, and Turkey. The Southern Exposition put Louisville back on the map as an industrialized city.

He also helped raise money to build the platform for the Statue of Liberty. After becoming a successful businessman, he used his money towards the improvements of his new adopted city of Louisville, Kentucky. He became a member of the first and second Boards of the Park Commissioners, which established the Louisville Park System in 1891-1895, and was president of the board in 1907-1908.

After the Civil War, Cowan became an advocate for peace. He wanted to heal the wounded between the Union and Confederate veterans. He was the founder of the Blue and Gray reunion at Gettysburg reunion in 1887, and in 1895 during the Grand Army of the Republic Reunion in Louisville, Kentucky, he wanted the theme of the reunion to be one of reconciliation and peace. In 1905, during the Confederate Reunion in Louisville, the Confederate veterans honored Cowan for his efforts for the care and welfare of his former combatants and made him the only honorary member of the Kentucky Orphan Brigade. Cowan was one of the most staunchest friends of the Confederate Home in Pee Wee Valley, Oldham County, Kentucky and donated gifts and took a personal interest in the welfare of the home. At the fiftieth anniversary of the Battle of Gettysburg Reunion, Cowan advocated a peace memorial at Gettysburg. Cowan also invited the Confederate Veterans to have their reunion in 1917 at Washington, D.C.

Cowan admired and honored President Abraham Lincoln and was on the board of the Lincoln memorial at Hodgenville, Kentucky. During the dedication of the cornerstone for the Lincoln memorial, Cowan helped coordinated the dedication ceremony.

He was in several military organizations, serving as president of the Grand Army of the Republic, president of the Society of the Army of the Potomac, 1911 to 1916, commander of the Ohio Commandery of the Military Order of the Loyal Legion from 1914 to 1916, and junior vice commander in chief of the same order from 1915 to 1918.

During his life, Cowan also was a philanthropist. He was a trustee of the American Printing House of the Blind, from 1897 to until his death, and president of the Kentucky Institute for the Education of the Blind from 1898 to 1900 and 1908 to 1918.[i] He was also a member of the Pendennis Club, Salmagundi Club, the Filson Historical Society, and the Conservation Club. He took an active part in Manual Training High School and was elected to the school board. Cowan was also a leader in the effort to secure a new site for a new Male High (Classical) School building and was one of the largest contributors to the fund. He was an organizer and charter member of the Council of the Charity Organization Society. He was a trustee of the Louisville Free Kindergarten Association. He was also a life member of the American Civil Association.

Cowan exhibited the best traits of an immigrant. He came to America with the high hopes of many immigrants who wanted a better life than their former homeland. Cowan received an education, fought bravely for his newly adopted country during the Civil War, became a successive businessman and amassed a fortune in his business of Andrew Cowan & Company. He felt so proud to being an American and Louisville inhabitant that he gave back to his country and community. He helped found the Louisville Parks System and gave to schools and institutions. The Civil War deeply affected him, and he devoted his life to peace and the mending of wounds between the Union and Confederate veterans. Cowan may have been seen as the hero of Gettysburg at the "Bloody Angle," but history may see Cowan as much more. Hopefully he will be seen as a shining beacon of Louisville's history and a peacemaker.

Colonel
ANDREW COWAN

Union Soldier, Louisville Citizen, Peacemaker

Chapter 1

Cowan Joins the Union Army

Andrew Cowan was born in Ayrshire, Scotland, on September 29, 1841. He was the son of William Strong and Margaret Lewis Isabella (Campbell). In 1848, Cowan's parents immigrated to the United States and settled in Auburn County, New York. In public schools, he received his early education and entered Madison University, now Colgate College, in Hamilton, New York. In the spring of 1860 during the Presidential election, Cowan remembered the Lincoln nomination by the Republican Party and had knowledge of the chagrin and sorrow that Lincoln's nomination brought to Cowan's friend, Governor William Seward of New York. Cowan stated that the campaign was the most exciting he had ever known. Cowan marched in the torchlight procession of the Little Giants in red capes, who were the supporters of the "Little Giant" Stephen Douglas, who ran for the Democratic ticket and with the "Railsplitters" in black who supported Republican candidate Abraham Lincoln. Cowan brought his mother the odor and stains of whale oil from the dripping campaign lamps. He banged the bell in the parades of John Bell and Edward Everett, who were running on the Constitutional Unionist Party. Cowan only saw the fun in the election campaigns and was too young to see the political strife the country was undergoing.[ii]

In April of 1861, Andrew Cowan was planning a trip home to accept an offer to run the telegraph office for a month in Auburn, but his plans changed when Confederate General P. G. T. Beauregard fired on Fort Sumter in the Charleston, South Carolina harbor. The Civil War had begun. United States President Abraham Lincoln called for 75,000 volunteers. The nineteen-year-old Cowan heeded the call of the President and decided to quit college and join the Union army. On April 16, 1861, he enlisted as a private in Captain Terrance Kennedy's company of riflemen, which became Company B, 19th New York State Volunteer Infantry. The state of New York issued the men antiquated smoothbore muskets. On May 23, 1861, at Elmira, New York, he mustered into service.[iii] The 19th New York proceeded to Washington, D.C., set up camp and began drilling. Cowan was elected First Sergeant, and served at Washington under Union General Robert Patterson.

While in Washington, D.C., Cowan camped on Kalorama Heights, now part of the National Capitol, but back then the Heights was a sun baked farm of red clay. His regiment was known as the Seward Regiment. In June of 1861, Lincoln visited Cowan's camp. When he heard the President was in camp, he ran to the colonel's quarters to see the President. Lincoln was surrounded by nearly a thousand men from his regiment and as he gazed at Lincoln, Cowan's heart sank, because he was very homely and seemed uncouth and without dignity. Lincoln shook hands left and right while sweat poured down his strong, homely face. In his hand was a plug hat, which was weather beaten and faded. Lincoln wore the hat tight above his brow. He wore an old faded linen duster coat, the same kind that travelers wore on rails or carriages. The coat made Lincoln's long, thin figure appear even more elongated, because he towered above all the other men. While Cowan watched and pressed closer to where he stood, the linen coat became saturated from the neck down to his waist and the outline of his suspenders became plainly visible. The President wore no vest. Cowan turned away without shaking his hand.[iv] The chance encounter with Lincoln would not be his last.

On August 23, the 19th New York assembled on the parade grounds, hoping that their ninety days enlist was up, but to Cowan's surprise, an artillery battery unlimbered at the edge of the field, two squads of cavalry rode up and halted on either side of the field and a regiment of Pennsylvania volunteers formed a line behind them. As the men stood in their ranks, Henry Stone, adjutant of the 19th New York, read an order from the Governor of New York, turning the 19th New York regiment over to the service of the Federal government for the unexpired term of its enlistment as a militia New York regiment for two years. He read another order from Union General Nathaniel Banks stating that anyone who refused the order would be sent to hard labor until the two years expired. Most of the 19th New York was in shock.[v] They now had to serve two years in the Union army.

In September of 1861, Kennedy and Cowan returned to Auburn to recruit additional men for the regiment. Both men traveled to Washington to make arrangement for their return to New York. Kennedy set up a meeting with Secretary of State William Seward, who was also from Auburn. Kennedy hoped that Seward would support his idea of raising an artillery battery in Cayuga County. Seward liked the idea and gave Kennedy his blessing in raising the battery. On October 13, 1861, the War Department gave Kennedy permission to raise a light battery within thirty days.[vi] As soon as Kennedy and Cowan arrived in Auburn, the men began recruiting for the 19th New York and the new battery. Cowan stated he went to work recruiting for the regiment, "but we kept the biggest recruits for the battery.[vii] Kennedy, Cowan, and the most prominent men in Auburn visited all the parts of Cayuga County, holding meetings in churches and town halls, asking for volunteers. Cowan called the recruitment drives the "Whirlwind Campaign."[viii]

By November of 1861, Kennedy, Cowan and 156 men of the new battery headed south. Kennedy was commissioned a captain of the First New York Independent Battery. On November 23, 1861, Cowan was commissioned a senior first lieutenant of the new battery. William Wright became a first lieutenant in the new battery, and the second lieutenants were William H. Johnson and James Orion Woodruff. On December 2, the men traveled to Albany, then boarded a steamer for New York City. By December 4, the men boarded railway cars and traveled to Philadelphia, then Baltimore, and by December 6, they arrived in Washington, D.C. The men were located at Camp Berry, located a half mile from the capital.[ix]

On January 13, 1862, the men of the First New York Independent Battery harnessed their horses and awaited orders to pick up their new cannons from the Navy yard. The battery was equipped with 3-inch ordnance rifles. The 3-inch ordnance rifled cannon was the most common field piece used in the Civil War. The United States War Department purchased the guns in 1861. The cannon were very maneuverable, accurate at long range, and capable of firing a wide range of shells. The wrought iron barrel weighed around 820 pounds and was constructed of sheets of boiler iron wrapped around a core. The sturdy tube did not need any type of breech reinforcement. The gun tapered evenly from breech to muzzle in a distinctive, sleek look. The bore was three inches and could fire elongated ten pound Schenkl, Hotchkiss, and Parrott shells. The powder weighed one pound and could propel a shell up to two thousand yards at an elevation of only five degrees. Greater distances could be achieved by increasing the elevations.[x] The men of the battery began to train on their new cannons, but unfortunately, they had no rounds to practice with; the artillery rounds would not arrive until two months later.[xi]

While in camp, disease ran rampant. Men of the 1st New York Independent Battery came down with measles and typhoid fever. Four men died from disease. By February the battery received orders to break ground and join General William Smith's division of the Army of the Potomac at Camp Griffin, Virginia. The divisional chief of artillery for Smith's division was Captain Romeyn B. Ayres. On February 12, 1862, the 1st New York received their first allotment of live ammunition, allowing them to fire their batteries for the first time.[xii] While in camp, Union commander Union George B. McClellan, commander of the Army of the Potomac, was formulating a plan to attack Richmond, Virginia, the new capital of the Confederacy. The Confederate capital had been moved from Montgomery, Alabama to Richmond. The upcoming campaign was known as the Peninsular Campaign and the 1st New York Independent Battery would experience their first taste of battle.

Chapter 2

The Battle of Williamsburg: The Peninsular Campaign

In early March of 1862, Union General George B. McClellan, commander of the Army of the Potomac, devised an amphibious expedition. His army would sail past Urbanna, Virginia, continue down the Chesapeake Bay and land on tip of the Virginia Peninsula. The men would land at Fort Monroe, and the fort would become a base for operations towards Richmond, Virginia. Fort Monroe was located seventy miles from Richmond. McClellan planned to move east against Richmond. Confederate General John B. Magruder and seventeen thousand Confederate soldiers were stretched out from Yorktown across the peninsula to the Warwick River. Nearly four hundred vessels transported McClellan's 121,500 men and forty-four batteries to Fort Monroe. McClellan planned on moving rapidly up the Peninsula. He decided to locate his base near West Point, near the head of the York River.[xiii]

McClellan's first major roadblock to Richmond was Yorktown. On April 4, McClellan began his advance on Yorktown. The Third Corps under Union Brigadier General Samuel Heintzelman, headed up the road directly toward Yorktown, while the IV Corps, under Union Brigadier General Erasmus Keyes, headed to the left in order to flank Yorktown. The Second Corps, under Brigadier General Edwin Sumner, followed in reserve on the Yorktown road.[xiv] The 1st New York Independent Battery was under the command of Captain Terrance Kennedy and attached to the IV Corps, 2nd Division, under the command of General William "Baldy" Smith. Smith's division comprised of the 1st Brigade under General Winfield Hancock, the 2nd brigade, under the command of General William Brooks, and the Third Brigade under General John Davidson. The Artillery brigade was under the command of General Romeyn Ayres. Ayres was a career army officer. He was born in Montgomery City, New York on December 20, 1825. He graduated from the United States Military Academy in 1847, ranking twenty-second in his class. His first assignment was the occupation forces in Puebla and Mexico City at the end of the Mexican War. After the Mexican War, he was sent to various frontier outposts and eastern garrisons. Before the Civil War broke out, he was a lieutenant in the 3rd Artillery for nearly a decade. On May 14, 1861, he was promoted to captain of the 5th United States Artillery, serving under Brigadier General Irvin McDowell at First Bull Run. On October 3, 1861, he was promoted to chief of artillery, Smith's Division, Army of the Potomac. By March of 1862, Ayres was promoted to chief of artillery, 2nd Division, 4th Corps, Army of the Potomac.[xv]

By April 5, 1862, General Heintzelman confronted Yorktown's earthworks, which were fifteen feet thick with ditches up to ten feet deep and fifteen feet wide. The Confederates located behind the earthworks began to fire upon Heintzelman's men. Keyes' corps came across the Warwick River. Confederates began to fire on Keyes's men on Lee's Mill Dam, six miles from Yorktown. Although McClellan could have taken the Confederates at the Warwick River, he hesitated, and thought there were one hundred thousand Confederates confronting him, which was extremely exaggerated. McClellan decided on a siege of Yorktown. While McClellan planned for a siege of Yorktown, the Confederates were able to send reinforcements. On April 16, McClellan sent Brigadier General William Smith, commander of the Second Division, IV Corps to conduct a reconnaissance mission at Burnt Chimney's, a dam located one mile north of Lee's mills. Smith sent Brigadier General William Brooks and five regiments to move to the edge of the Warwick River. The Union troops drove the Confederates from their rifle pits, and three companies charged over the mill dam, while four companies crossed the river at the ford. Confederate reinforcements under General Howell Cobb counterattacked, so Smith withdrew his men. On April 17, Confederate General Joseph Johnston arrived at Yorktown and the numbers at Yorktown swelled to fifty thousand men.[xvi] Johnston placed his men near Fair Oaks Station on the Richmond & York River Railroad and near the town of Seven Pines.

The 1st New York Independent Battery experienced a command change before the battery moved out with Hancock toward Williamsburg. Captain Terrance Kennedy resigned as commander of the 1st New York in order to take the rank of major and command the 3rd New York Independent Battery. Cowan was promoted to captain and took command of the 1st New York. Cowan immediately took command of the battery.[xvii]

On May 3, 1862, McClellan moved one hundred and fourteen siege guns at Yorktown, including three hundred field pieces, and on May 5 he planned to bombard Yorktown. Confederate General Joseph Johnston decided to withdraw from Yorktown. The Confederates decided to retreat towards Williamsburg, located twelve miles to the west. General Magruder had built earthworks at Williamsburg. He had thirteen redoubts and they stretched for four miles across the narrow neck of the Peninsula. The flanks were covered by creeks and marshes. The largest of the redoubts was Fort Magruder. On May 4, that same day, General Smith's division of the IV Corps stopped in front of Fort Magruder and he awaited orders from General Sumner. General Joseph Hooker's III Corps arrived and took a position on Smith's left. General Sumner sent in General Philip Kearney's division of the III Corps. Kearney's men forced the Confederates back.[xviii]

General Sumner sent Union General Winfield Hancock's two thousand five hundred men to a flanking movement towards two empty redoubts. Hancock ordered four or five volunteers from each regiment of his brigade to cross the creek and take the chance that the redoubts were evacuated. Sumner also ordered Hancock to take three regiments to cover his front, and follow the volunteers across the dam. By the time he was ready to cross, General Brooks had determined that the redoubts were empty and Hancock's men immediately occupied the works. Hancock ordered the 5th Wisconsin, the 43rd New York, and the 49th New York to advance. When Hancock arrived at Lebanon, his brigade was ordered to halt. General Smith took command and ordered Hancock's brigade to Williamsburg. The Confederates had set on fire the bridge over Skiff Creek, and when his cavalry tried to extinguish the flames, the Confederates opened fire. Hancock sent four companies of the 2nd Vermont to the burning bridge and ordered them to extinguish the flames. The Vermont infantry put out the flames and drove off the enemy. At 3:00 p.m., Hancock arrived near the Whittaker's house, where General Stoneman and the artillery were engaged with the Confederates. At 5:30 p.m., Hancock formed a line of battle, two of his regiments on the right of the road and two on the left. General Smith and General Sumner arrived on the scene and directed the battle. General Brooks' brigade arrived and formed a second line of battle. Hancock made room for the Third Brigade. General Sumner ordered an assault on the works. The First brigade advanced, followed by General Brooks' brigade. Hancock advanced with his men and found the woods to be thick and tangled, and the assault was brought to a halt until daylight the next day. During the night, rain poured down the roads.[xix]

On May 5, at 11:00 a.m., Hancock met with General Sumner, who ordered him to take four or five regiments of infantry and a battery of artillery and cross Cub Dam Creek and take position of the Confederate works on the opposite side of the creek commanding the dam. According to reports, the works had been abandoned by the Confederates. Hancock ordered the 5th Wisconsin, 49th Pennsylvania, 6th Maine, 7th Maine, 33rd New York, and Cowan's battery of six 3-inch ordnance guns to accompany his advance. Hancock emerged out of the woods in open country, with the York River in view. Hancock turned to the left and came in view of the earthwork overlooking the dam. At this time, General Keyes appeared in view of the earthwork and called for Hancock. Hancock placed Cowan's artillery in battery on the crest of the hill about six hundred yards in front of the first rebel earthworks. Hancock sent the 5th Wisconsin and the 6th Maine across the dam and into the works. Finding the fort unoccupied, Hancock left a garrison of the 33rd New York to protect his rear infantry. At 12 noon, Hancock sent a message to General Keyes and Smith that he had crossed the Cub Creek Dam. Hancock advanced and took another unoccupied redoubt. Hancock advanced to the next two redoubts occupied by the Confederates and created a diversion, to relieve pressure on General Hooker.[xx]

At 7:30 a.m., Hooker attacked the Confederates. Guns from Battery H, 1st U. S. Artillery and 6th New York Battery opened up on Fort Magruder. Hooker's men advanced on Fort Magruder. Confederate General James Longstreet's six brigades counterattacked and drove Hooker back. By 4:00 p.m., Union General Philip Kearney mounted another attack against Fort Magruder. His attack forced Longstreet's men back into Fort Magruder and the surrounding redoubts, but the Union forces could not break the Rebel line. The Federals under Kearny fell back a mile and a half from Fort Magruder.[xxi]

While Hooker and Kearny were battling Fort Magruder, Andrew Cowan's artillery moved forward and came upon a Confederate redoubt. Union General Winfield Hancock ordered Cowan to open fire upon the Confederate redoubt some 1,200 yards to his front and left. After throwing twenty shells and case shot, he moved forward and placed two of his cannons on the right and four on the left of the road about three hundred and fifty yards from the Confederate redoubt. The

Confederates brought two or three pieces to fire on Cowan's guns from the woods. The Confederates had excellent range on Cowan's guns. Luckily, the Confederate shells failed to explode. Cowan directed two of his pieces to fire on the rebel artillery and three of his guns on the rebel earthworks.[xxii]

During this time, Captain C.C. Wheeler, commanding Battery E, First New York Artillery, unlimbered to the right of Cowan between the Confederate barracks. With the combined artillery of Cowan and Wheeler, Hancock had ten pieces firing down on the Confederate forces. Captain Cowan lost one man, Private Edmund Terry, who was killed by a six-pound shot while manning his gun in the number one position, and Lucas Goodyear was slightly injured by a 12-pound spent shell that struck him on the shoulder and side. The Confederates withdrew their artillery to a more secure position in their rear.[xxiii]

At 5:10 p.m., the clouds opened up and rain fell on the battlefield. Hancock was just about to give the order to fall back, when he observed the Confederates placing infantry into redoubts on his front and his skirmishers were firing on them. A column of Confederate cavalry came out of the woods near the redoubt to the right. The Union skirmishers fired on the Confederate cavalry to within four hundred yards. The Confederates planned to attack the artillery, so Hancock ordered Cowan and Wheeler to fire shell and to retire to his second line. Confederate infantry had gone into the woods to try and flank Hancock's men. Confederate General Jubal Early and General Daniel Hill asked permission to attack Hancock's 1,600 men with their 2,700 men. Hancock observed the Rebel infantry break through the woods in front of his right flank. Hancock ordered two regiments on the left of the Cowan and Wheeler to fall back in line of battle to the crest on the left of the redoubt.[xxiv]

The 6th Maine, the nearest to the battery, fell back to the crest and halted and waited for their skirmishers, who were engaging the Confederates on the left redoubt. In the meantime, the 49th Pennsylvania, on the left of the 6th Maine, retreated until the regiment came to the crest, when the regiment halted. The 6th Maine fell back to the crest and formed a perfect line as the 49th Pennsylvania. The 5th Wisconsin, which was on the right of the battery, formed a square to resist the Confederate cavalry attack. Although Cowan's artillery and skirmishers held back the Confederate cavalry attack, Confederate infantry, which had broken through the woods, advanced on the regiment, so

Hancock ordered the 5th Wisconsin to fall back in line of battle. After the last piece of artillery threw several rounds of canister into the Confederates at a range of one hundred yards, they limbered up and fell back to the second position.

The 5th Wisconsin fell back in the direction of the redoubt. Hancock ordered the 7th Maine to fall back to their original line, with their right against the woods, to be able to meet any assault from that direction. Hancock withdrew three companies of the 33rd New York and formed them on the left of the 7th Maine, placing a portion of his artillery between the regiment and the redoubt. Because of the rain soaked roads, Hancock had difficulty placing his artillery into position on the right and left of the redoubt. Cowan wrote that his guns "were sunk nearly to the hubs"[xxv] and he had difficulty bringing the guns off the field and into position. Cowan stated that the ground was so "heavy that it was difficult for the horses to draw the pieces."[xxvi] Private James Neville and Levi Cleveland, under the command of Cowan, were slightly wounded while bringing the guns off the field. Hancock ordered his artillery to a third position on the plain between his infantry and the dam. Hancock directed four companies of the 6th Maine into the redoubt. Hancock waited until the 5th Wisconsin, already being attacked by the Confederates, to get into position before he ordered attack on the Rebels. When the advance companies of the 5th Wisconsin reached the crest, he formed a part of them on the left of the redoubt, on the same ground from which he had taken the four companies of the 6th Maine, to garrison the work, and formed the remainder behind the crest on the right of the redoubt.

The Confederates advanced to within thirty paces of Hancock's men. Hancock ordered a forward movement to the crest. The whole line advanced, cheering, and when they arrived at the top of the crest, they fired two volleys into the Rebels and Hancock gave the order to charge down the slope and the whole command advanced. A few of the Confederates were bayonetted, but most broke and fled. Hancock ordered his men to halt at the foot of the slope and delivered "a terrible fire along the whole line, expending fifteen to twenty rounds. The plunging fire from the redoubt the direct fire from the right, and the oblique fire from the left were so destructive that after it had been ordered to cease and the smoke arose it seemed that no man had left the ground unhurt who had advanced within five hundred yards of our line."[xxvii] Hancock stated that "the enemy were completely routed and dispersed."

During the battle, General Early was wounded in the shoulder. The second Confederate line came to a halt. Hancock directed his artillery under Cowan and Wheeler to fire a few shells at the second line, when Confederates disappeared. The Confederate regiment on Hancock's left flank faded into the woods and retreated. Without reinforcements, Hancock decided to hold his position and not pursue the retreating Rebels. According to Hancock, the 5th North Carolina was annihilated, with nearly all of their superior officers left dead or wounded on the field. The 24th Virginia also suffered in the loss of superior officers and men. One of the Confederate battle flags was captured by the 5th Wisconsin.[xxviii] During the battle, Hancock lost 10 killed, 88 wounded, and 31 missing.

After nightfall, General A.J. Smith ordered Cowan to place three guns on the left of the upper work and two on the right of the center. In his official report on the Battle of Williamsburg, General Hancock, commanding the First Brigade, gave Cowan the highest recommendation. Hancock had won the battle and received the highest praise from McClellan.

The Battle of Williamsburg cost the Confederates 1,703 men killed, wounded, and missing, out of 30,000 men. The Federals suffered 456 men killed, 1,410 wounded, and 373 missing, out of a force of forty thousand men. Richmond was now only fifty miles away.

During the night, Confederate General Joseph Johnston decided to abandon Williamsburg. Johnston accomplished his mission of delaying the Federals from pursuing the Confederates long enough so they could withdraw up the peninsula toward Richmond.

On May 15, at Drewry's Bluff, only seven miles from Richmond, the Confederates were able to place river obstructions and cannons to halt a Union flotilla from attacking Richmond. On May 31, rains washed away bridges over the Chickahominy and isolated the III and IV Corps, under Generals Samuel Heintzelman and Erasmus Keyes near the villages of Seven Pines and Fair Oaks Station. On May 31, Johnson attacked the Union troops at Fair Oaks or Seven Pines and his intricate battle plans led to a lack of coordination and confusion. At the battle of Fair Oaks, while riding along the battle lines, General Johnston fell severely wounded from a shell. President Jefferson Davis replaced Johnston with Confederate General Robert E. Lee. McClellan's soldiers held their ground in a tactical victory.[xxix]

By the third week of June, the Chickahominy still cut McClellan's army in half. McClellan left only General Fitz-John Porter's V Corps on the northern side of the river in an exposed position. On June 26, Lee attacked Porter at Beaver Dam Creek. General A.P. Hill's sixteen thousand Confederates attacked Porter near Beaver Dam Creek. Nightfall ended the attack. Hill lost 1,400 killed and wounded. Porter held his ground. During the night, McClellan abandoned the line of Beaver Dam Creek without further fighting. Lee again attacked Porter at Gaines Mill. During the battle, Porter's line collapsed under the Confederate assault and withdrew to the bridges over the Chickahominy. Lee attacked Porter near Gaines' Mill. Porter withdrew to the bridges over the Chickahominy and crossed his army to the other side, leaving 6,800 men killed, wounded, or captured. Lee lost 9,000 men.

On the other side of the river, McClellan's army remained inactive. Lee strengthened Richmond's defenses while McClellan slowly approached the city. Cowan stated that he could see the church spires in Richmond. Confederate General J. E. B. Stuart's cavalry rode completely around the Union army. McClellan's right flank was unsecured and convinced McClellan that he was outnumbered. Lee positioned twenty-five thousand Confederate soldiers between Richmond and McClellan. McClellan thought he was outnumbered, decided to save his army and ordered a withdrawal to the James River, and head for the safety of Harrison's Landing.[xxx] The Union army, along with Cowan's battery, marched day and night. On July 1, Confederate General Robert E. Lee ordered a final attack in an effort to defeat the Federals. The Army of the Potomac turned and gave battle to Lee at Malvern Hill. Cowan wrote that the Union army had the advantage of position and their great train of artillery was finally to have their day on the field. Cowan witnessed as Confederate General Magruder's infantry repeatedly charged across the fields almost to the foot of the right where the Union cannons poured their iron hell. Cowan stated that the Charge of the Light Brigade at the Battle of Balaklava "was a summer breeze to the fierce tropical hurricane" unleased by the Union artillery.[xxxi] Lee's defeat at the battle of Malvern Hill concluded the Peninsular Campaign. The Army of the Potomac won the battle, and by night, both armies were exhausted. At midnight, McClellan pulled his army off the battlefield in the rain and thunder and began the march to Harrison's Landing.[xxxii]

When McClellan's army arrived at Harrison's Landing, there was no place for Cowan's artillerymen to rest, except to lie down in a sea of mud, churned by the wheels of thousands of wagons that had come before the troops. The Army of the Potomac was tired and demoralized. The army quickly recovered their strength and spirit and had constructed a line of rifle pits and redoubts. The Army was safe and secure in their new position. President Lincoln came from Washington to see for himself whether the rumors concerning the Army of the Potomac were true.[xxxiii]

The review of the army was ordered by General McClellan, and Cowan was to see the President for the second time during his career. The army paraded standing in their rifle pits and redoubts, where the reviewing officers rode out in front of the line of entrenchments. Cowan stood on the parapets of the redoubt occupied by the guns of the battery which he commanded, so that he was able to see the reviewing party riding from the left, long before the commanding officer was abreast of Cowan. Cowan saw General McClellan's staff, with foreign princes and dukes and military attaches from all European countries, and then a regiment of lancers, each man carrying a lance with a red pennant waving from its point. Cowan remarked that the reviewing party was a "very brilliant spectacle." The President held the reins in his left hand without pressing on the horse's mouth, like an accomplished rider, and his sat on his horse with ease, "like a boy who had learned to ride bareback." He was dressed in black broadcloth, like a preacher, and in his right hand was a shiny new silk hat, which he waved as Cowan's men cheered him, and his face was smiling and kind as he looked toward Cowan's men. Cowan stated that Lincoln rode "with kingly grace and I would then have given my shoulder straps for the privilege of grasping his hand."[xxxiv]

Chapter 3

The Battle of Antietam

On September 7, 1862, Confederate General Robert E. Lee and forty thousand men from the Army of Northern Virginia crossed the Potomac River. Lee's invasion hoped to acquire food for his army from the fall harvest, recruit thousands of Maryland volunteers, and earn European diplomatic recognition for the Confederacy. The Rebel soldiers massed at Frederick, Maryland. While at Frederick, Lee issued Order No. 191, which divided the army. Lee planned to move his army north into Pennsylvania. General Thomas "Stonewall" Jackson would open a supply line into the Shenandoah Valley against the Union garrison at Harpers Ferry. After capturing the Union force, Jackson would reunite with General James Longstreet's three divisions and move north.[xxxv]

On September 4, 1862, the Union government learned of Lee's invasion, at a time when the Union army suffered a defeat by Lee's army at the Second Battle of Bull Run just five days before. President Lincoln decided to place in command General George B. McClellan once again to meet the Confederate invasion. McClellan reorganized the army and marched towards the Confederate forces. Andrew Cowan's battery was assigned to the VI Corps, 2nd Division, under General William "Baldy" Smith. Smith's division contained the 1st Brigade under General Winfield Hancock, the 2nd Brigade under the command of General William Brooks, and the 3rd Brigade under Colonel William Irvin. The Chief of Artillery for the VI Corps was Captain Romeyn Ayres. Along with Cowan's 1st Independent Battery, the artillery brigade was comprised of the Maryland Light, Battery B, under Lt. Theodore Vannerman, and the 5th United States Battery F, under Lt. Leonard Martin. McClellan had 84,000 men advance slowly toward Frederick, but on September 11, he learned that the Confederates had left Frederick and captured Hagerstown. On September 13, McClellan arrived at Frederick. To McClellan's amazement, he was handed a copy of Lee's Order 191 to his commanders detailing the divided Confederate army movements. The orders were discovered by two Union soldiers, who found the orders wrapped around two cigars. McClellan now had Lee's entire battle plans.[xxxvi]

On September 14, the Union IX Corps entered Fox's Gap and the Confederate forces under Confederate General Daniel Hill fought against the oncoming Union troops. A mile north at Boonsborough Gap, the Union I Corps attacked the Confederate defenders. Hill redirected his five brigades against the Union soldiers. The arrival of Longstreet's other two divisions saved the Confederates from a rout. The Confederates lost 2,700 men and the Union army lost 1,800 men. Five miles to the south, General William Franklin's VI Corps marched into Crampton's Gap but stopped advancing when they became engaged with Confederate soldiers, and eventually the Confederate center broke, but Franklin halted his men, instead of obeying McClellan's orders to relieve Harpers Ferry.[xxxvii]

On September 15, General Jackson captured Harpers Ferry. Colonel Dixon Miles, the garrison commander, was killed. Over 10,000 men, 13,000 weapons, and 73 cannon fell into Rebel hands. Lee's plans were altered and he decided to concentrate his forces at Sharpsburg. The next day on September 16, Lee gathered his forces at Antietam Creek. McClellan moved onto the field and formulated his plan of attack the next day. He pushed his two corps west across the Antietam Creek. McClellan had 75,000 Federal troops facing Lee's 40,000 men.[xxxviii]

On Wednesday morning September 17, 1862, McClellan told his generals he planned to strike both Confederate flanks while maintaining a reserve to break the Confederate center. Union General Joseph Hooker looked through his field glasses and saw in an open area a mile away in front of the Dunker church Confederate artillery. McClellan ordered Hooker to attack the left of the Rebel position at Sharpsburg, with the capture of the batteries as his objective. Confederate Colonel Stephen D. Lee commanded twenty-six pieces of artillery in front of the Dunker church. Confederate General Stonewall Jackson's 7,000 men and Hooker's 8,600 men faced each other across the field.

The battle began at first light, with Hooker's three division I Corps marching through a cornfield bordering the turnpike and pushing Jackson's line back into the woods north of the Dunker church. A Confederate counterattack pushed the Union troops back through the cornfield. The Confederates were attacked by the XII Corps under the command of General Joseph Mansfield. The Confederate batteries in front of Dunker Church ran low on ammunition and fell back across the pike to refill their caissons with ammunition. Mansfield was mortally wounded during the attack, but the 7,200 men in his XII Corps fought their way through the cornfield and massed around the church. Jackson's men fell back and managed to hold off the Union assault until reinforcements arrived. Hooker attempted to gather the remnants of his I Corps for another attack, when a sniper's bullet hit his right foot. Hooker was carried to the rear. The I Corps was scattered, the XII lost twenty-five percent of their force, and the Confederates waited for reinforcements. Firing stopped on the battlefield. By 9:00 a.m., over eight thousand men, both Union and Confederate, laid across the blood soaked battlefield. The first part of the battle was over.[xxxix]

At 7:20 a.m., Confederate General John Bell Hood counterattacked from the West Woods, and Union General Sumner's II Corps advanced to meet Hood. Sumner led General John Sedgwick and General William French across the Antietam Creek, with the intention of attacking the West Woods, turn the Confederate left flank and run south towards the town of Sharpsburg. During the advance, General French was not able to catch up with Sumner and linked up with General Greene's division from the XII Corps. Sumner's 5,400 men attacked the West Woods. The Federal left was exposed and attacked from three directions by Lee's reinforcements. Sumner's men ran back across the fields with the Confederates close in hot pursuit. The Union cannons under the I and XII Corps fired into the oncoming Confederates. The directed artillery fire stopped the Confederate assault, and the Rebels crossed back over the fields to resume their positions in the West Woods.[xl]

By 10:00 a.m., Sumner ordered General George Gordon's XII Corps brigade to advance through the cornfield, but were stopped by Confederate General Walker's men firing from the West Woods. The Union troops stopped at a fence rail north of Dunker Church. Two of Greene's brigades rose up and fired at two Confederate assaults from the church. Greene drove the Rebels back into the woods but chased after them, pushing about two hundred yards into the woods behind Dunker Church before stopping and calling for reinforcements. McClellan did not send reinforcements and the battle stopped on the Confederate left.[xli]

The battle began to progress from the West Woods around Dunker Church to the Confederate center, where Confederate General Daniel H. Hill's division were located. His men took a position in a salient formed by an old farm road that had been worn down by wagons to the point where the road was several feet below the level of the surrounding area. The road formed a natural trench. Hill's men strengthened the trench by adding breastworks made of fence rails. The road became known as the Sunken Road. Confederate General James Longstreet commanded the Confederate center, with General D.H. Hill's division of 2,500 men at the center. A low ridge fifty to eighty yards in front of and parallel to the road kept the Union attackers and Hill's men from seeing each other. Hill's men waited for Union General William French's division, which consisted of 5,700 men. French's men charged with their bayonets. The Rebels waited until French's men were within a couple yards then unleashed rifle fire. The entire front line went down and the Federal troops fell back and took cover behind a crest. French's other two brigades crested the ridge and met the same fate and fell back. Over 1,500 Union soldiers lay dead on the battlefield. French lost one third of his command trying to take the Sunken Lane.[xlii]

General Israel Richardson's division of four thousand men was the next division to assault Hill's position. Confederate General Richard Anderson's division reinforced Hill's men. Richardson's assault caught the Rebels at the right moment when their lines were thrown into confusion. The commander of the one brigade had pulled his men back out of the confused mass of troops in the Sunken Road, and nearby regiments, thinking the entire position was being abandoned, decided to climb out of the Sunken Road and ran towards the rear. At the same time a junior officer at the other end of the line misunderstood his orders to pull back one flank of his regiment and withdrew the entire regiment. Nearby regiments thought the withdrawal signaled a general retreat and they abandoned their section of the line. The Confederates who decided to stay and defend the Sunken Road were torn to pieces from flanking Union fire and the lane filled with dead and wounded. The Sunken Road became the Bloody Lane. Richardson's men surged forward and fired into the backs of the retreating Confederates. The center of the Confederate lines had collapsed and the Confederates fell back to a new line along the Hagerstown Turnpike, some six hundred yards to the rear. The Confederates amassed cannons and they held their position for the rest of the day.[xliii]

As firing subsided on the Sunken Road, the battlefield shifted to a stone bridge on the Federal left flank. The Rohrback's bridge would later be called Burnside's bridge, after Union General Ambrose Burnside. McClellan ordered General Burnside's IX Corps to cross the bridge as a diversion, while Union General Joseph Hooker launched his main attack. Confederate General Robert Toombs brigade faced General Burnside's eleven thousand men. Toombs had twelve artillery pieces. Burnside decided to attack Toomb's men by assaulting the bridge and fording the Antietam a half-mile downstream. Burnside attempted to take the bridge three times. Colonel Edward Ferrero's 51st New York and the 51st Pennsylvania Regiments led the third assault across the bridge. Two Federal batteries moved upstream where they were able to place their guns to enfilade the Confederates across the bridge. Crook's men placed a light howitzer, which began to fire double canister across the creek. The Federal troops managed to move within twenty-five yards from the Confederates. By 1:00 p.m., the Federals rushed the bridge and the Confederate troops withdrew up the hill. Burnside lost five hundred men. Confederate forces only lost 160 men. The 51st Pennsylvania and the 51st New York crossed the bridge and were followed by the rest of General Sturgis division.[xliv]

By 3:00 p.m., Burnside's entire corps was across the Antietam and ready to advance. The plan was to block Confederate General Lee's line of retreat west of Sharpsburg. While Burnside's men marched toward Sharpsburg, Confederate General Ambrose P. Hill's Confederate soldiers attacked Burnside's flank, forcing the Union soldiers back to Antietam Creek. The battlefield became silent while Hill consulted his officers. Hill's attack broke the Federal left. Cox ordered a withdrawal. Burnside and Cox fell back to the west bank of the Antietam, to the heights overlooking the bridge. By 5:30 p.m., the battle of Antietam was over. McClellan did not want to attack the Confederates any longer, and General A.P. Hill was outnumbered, so he also did not want to counterattack.

During the Battle of Antietam, Major General William Smith's division, along with Cowan's battery, marched towards Sharpsburg. Smith's division crossed the creek and occupied a position to where the Union right was engaged. Smith went down the hill towards the Pry house, crossed the Antietam ford and came up in the rear of General Sumner's right and ordered to form him division near the rear of the batteries on the extreme right. The division was behind and right of the East Woods. Before forming his division, Lieutenant Colonel Joseph Taylor of Sumner's staff rode up to Smith and informed him that a battery on the right center was unsupported and he ordered two brigades from General Hancock's brigade to support the battery. Hancock ordered the remaining two regiments and two batteries, Cowan's 1st New York Independent and Lieutenant Theodore Vanneman's Battery B, Maryland Light Artillery, forward to support the battery. Cowan's battery rode through the East Woods. Major Francis N. Clark, the chief of artillery for the Second Corps, led the guns into position. He placed the guns on the crest of a hilly field just of the left of the 49th Pennsylvania Infantry, east of the D. R. Miller farm and north of the cornfield. Vanneman's battery relieved Knaps's battery. Cowan took position with Union General Winfield Scott Hancock's 1st Brigade on the field.

Hancock placed his regiments to support three batteries. Cowan's battery was to the right of the 49th Pennsylvania, the 43rd New York and a detachment of the 137th Pennsylvania between Cowan's guns and Frank's battery, the 6th Maine and the 5th Wisconsin Infantry, between Frank's and Cothran's battery, with the whole force being parallel to the woods in their front.[xlv] A Confederate battery located in the West Woods opened on Cowan as soon as he unlimbered. He returned fire. General Hancock rode up to the 49th Pennsylvania and asked why they were there. The men of the 49th Pennsylvania informed Hancock that the officer in charge of their company, Major Hurling, placed them in position, and headed to the rear. Hancock sent for Hurling, and cursed Hurling to get out in front of his men, then ordered the regiment to retire. As the last of the troops headed to the rear, Hancock rode over to Cowan. He removed a flask from his pocket, and Hancock took a sip, slipped the flask back into his pocket and turned to Cowan saying: "Now, Captain, let them have it!"[xlvi] Cowan commenced firing at the Confederate battery, and after two hours of firing, he compelled the Rebel battery to leave the field. During the time he had been engaged, another rebel battery farther to the left brought a partial cross-fire on Cowan's position. He directed his fire on the Confederate gun and silenced the battery. At 4:00 p.m., the Confederates brought up two pieces on his right in a cornfield, and opened on Union General

Edwin Sumner's batteries. Cowan changed his front to fire to the right and prevent the possibility of a cross fire. Union General Edwin Sumner's shells did not reach the Confederate guns, so Cowan opened fire. The Rebels fired less than six rounds a piece, limbered up, and retired. Nothing further occurred that day, except Cowan threw an occasional shell into the woods when he saw a considerable Confederate body of men moving in the woods.[xlvii] The following day, the battery remained in position, watching the Confederates across the field. The next day, as the Federal army, including Cowan's battery, advanced over the ground in pursuit of the Confederates, one of Cowan's men noticed the Confederate battery they had engaged on the day of the battle. Laid across the field were twelve dead horses, and two limber chests that had exploded and a broken wheel which showed signs of one gun having been dismounted from the carriage, while the ground was plowed with Union shells, and the ground soaked with blood.[xlviii]

The Battle of Antietam was the single bloodiest day in American history. Over 23,000 men were killed, wounded, or missing. One out of every four soldiers engaged were lost. On September 18, McClellan received 14,000 additional troops, giving him twice the number of Confederate's soldiers, but he refused to attack. Lee marched a few miles to the Potomac River and crossed over Boteler's Ford, near Shepherdstown, West Virginia into Virginia's Shenandoah Valley. During the battle, one third of McClellan's 75,000 men never fired a shot.

Chapter 4

The Battle of Fredericksburg

On November 7, 1862, Major General Ambrose Burnside replaced General George B. McClellan as commander of the Army of the Potomac. On November 15, 1862, Union General Ambrose Burnside's 130,000 men marched out to defeat Confederate General Robert E. Lee's Confederate Army of Northern Virginia and to capture Richmond, Virginia. Cowan's battery remained in the VI Corps, under the command Major General William F. Smith. Smith's 2nd Division was under the command of General Albion Howe. The brigade contained the 1st Brigade under the command of General Calvin Pratt, the 2nd Brigade, under Colonel Henry Whiting, and the 3rd Brigade under General Francis Vinton, Colonel Robert Taylor and final Thomas Neil. The artillery brigade contained Cowan's 1st New York Independent Battery, Battery B, Maryland Light, under Captain Alonzo Snow, 3rd Battery, New York Light, under Lt. William Harn, and the Battery F, 5th United States Battery, under Lt. Leonard Martin. Two days later, Burnside's army reached the heights above the Rappahannock River across from the town of Fredericksburg. Burnside planned to cross the river on pontoon bridges, but the pontoon trains arrived late. By the time the pontoon arrived, Confederate General Lee adjusted his movements to match Burnside's plans. Lee concentrated his 78,000 men in the town of Fredericksburg and a ridge of hills extending from above the Falmouth ford to Massaponax River, five miles below. The ridge formed an angle with the river, passing behind the town and overlooked by another ridge behind. Between the ridge and the river extended the plain on which the town of Fredericksburg stood. At 12:00 a.m., on December 11, 1862, Union engineers began placing the pontoons on the river across from Fredericksburg. The engineers hoped to construct two bridges quickly over the river in order for Burnside's massive army to cross the river and attack the Confederate army.[xlix]

General Burnside ordered General Henry Hunt, Chief of Artillery for the Army of the Potomac, to place the artillery to protect the construction of the bridges and to cover the passage of the army. Hunt had the task to cover the Confederate movements on the plain, to reply and silence the Rebel batteries along the crest of their ridge, to command the town, to cover and protect the building of the bridges and the crossing of the Union troops, and to protect the left flank of the army from attacks in the direction of the Massaponax River. Hunt had to cover the entire length with artillery. Henry Hunt was the driving force in welding the Army of the Potomac's artillery into a superb organization. He was born in Michigan in 1819, and entered West Point from Ohio after being orphaned. When he graduated from West Point in 1839, he was posted to the artillery and in the Mexican War he suffered one wound and earned two brevets. In one battle, he charged with a field piece right into the face of the enemy's works and at pointblank range demolished a Mexican gun. Along with William F. Berry and William F. French, he sat on a board that completely revised the theories of field artillery tactics, which became the Union army's artillery practice during the Civil War. At the Battle of Bull Run, he was commander of the 2nd United States Artillery, Battery M. With his four cannons, he covered the withdrawal of the Union army from an exposed position at Blackburn's Ford. After the battle, he was assigned to a staff position and given charge of organizing the batteries in the Washington, D.C. defenses. By the time of the Peninsular Campaign, he was commanding the artillery reserve and at Malvern Hill he proved the effectiveness of his batteries. One hundred cannons tore into Magruder's charging infantry and played a major role in their defeat. At Antietam, McClellan chose Hunt as his chief artillerist. Now Hunt was in command at Fredericksburg.[1]

Hunt placed his 147 guns. To the right, the cannons were under the command of Lieutenant Colonel Hays, which extended from Falmouth Dam to a deep long ravine, about five hundred yards below Falmouth. The right center was under the command of Colonel Charles Tompkins, First Rhode Island Artillery, which extended from the ravine to near the point assigned for the middle bridge. The left center was under the command of Colonel R.O. Tyler, First Connecticut Artillery, who occupied the crest of the ridge, commencing near the middle bridge and extending to a wooded ravine, near the center of the ridge. The left, under the command of Captain G. A. DeRussy, 4th U. S. Artillery, occupied the remainder of the crest of the high ridge, and the whole of the low ridge, terminating at Pollock's Mill. Cowan's battery was under the command of Captain De Russy. The left comprised of four 20 pounders, under the 5th New York Battery; four 20 pounders under Battery C, 1 New York Battalion; six three-inch ordnance rifles under the 1st Maryland; six three-inch ordnance rifles under the 2nd Maine; six three-inch ordnance rifles under Cowan; four three-inch ordnance rifles, Battery L, 1st New York; four three-inch ordnance rifles under the 4th Pennsylvania Battery; four three-inch ordnance rifles under Company F, 1st Pennsylvania; and four three-inch ordnance rifles under Battery G, 1st Pennsylvania.[li]

Burnside ordered all the batteries, first, to concentrate their fire on the Rebel works or guns, should the guns open fire on the Union troops crossing the river; second, to turn their fire upon Rebel troops should they oppose the crossing; third, to cover the deployment of the Union troops when across, by stopping the advance of the Rebels; and fourth, to aid the Union advance, when possible, by sweeping the ground in front of them with their fire. By 11:00 a.m., all the batteries were placed in position.

On December 11, before daylight, the engineers began the construction of the bridges and as the sunlight arose across the heights, the upper and middles bridges were about half constructed. A heavy fire of musketry opened up on the engineers from the opposite bank, which after considerable loss, drove the engineers off the bridges at both places. At 7:00 a.m., De Russy ordered three batteries, Cowan's, Amsden's, and Rickett's, to change their position to the riverbank, near the pontoon bridges, with the purpose of protecting the bridge working parties and the crossing of the Union troops. Cowan opened fire upon some of the buildings on the opposite side from which the rebel sharpshooters were firing on the Union engineer party. Not only did Cowan's battery fire, but the entire line of Union guns opened up and partially silenced the Rebel fire. A severe cannonade opened up on the Rebel sharpshooters hidden among the buildings at Fredericksburg. After the Rebel sharpshooters were silenced, another attempt was made to complete the bridges, but the Confederate skirmishers and a column of infantry moved down the street toward the water. A Union battery drove the Confederate infantry back, but the sharpshooters succeeded in stopping the work on the bridges, and the Union artillery could not open fire as long as the Union engineers worked on the bridges. General Burnside ordered the batteries to turn and fire on the town. Again the rebel sharpshooters were beaten down by the artillery. With the Rebels silenced, the Union engineers began their work, but a few hundred sharpshooters, scattered among the cellars, ditches, and behind stone walls, drove the engineers from the bridges.

At 2:30 p.m., Hunt proposed a plan to use flat bottomed rowboats, fill the boats with infantry, and have the men row to the opposite side of the river and attack the Rebels in their cover. The men would also row the pontoons to their places and complete the bridges. The artillery was again brought into action at both bridges and under the guns under the command of Colonel Charles Thompkins at the upper bridge and Major Doull at the middle bridge, the Union guns opened fire, silencing the Rebel fire. When the signal was given, the Union boats pushed across the river. The men from the 7th Michigan Infantry and 89th New York jumped out of the boats and charged the Rebels, driving them from their cover and capturing over eighty prisoners. At the lower bridge, De Russy's division, including Cowan's guns, were brought near the bridges, and drove off the Rebel sharpshooters, who tried to prevent the cutting down of the banks, to form a practicable road for artillery. During the remainder of the day, Cowan fired several shots at parties of Confederate troops. The ground was muddy and Cowan's three guns became disabled, when recoil broke the axles. At sunset, he threw a few shells into the buildings immediately after Union troops crossed the bridge.[lii]

At early daylight on December 12, Cowan's, Amsden's, and Rickett's batteries returned to their positions. Most of the day was spent crossing the Union troops and their batteries. At the upper batteries, General Sumner's division, with ten batteries crossed, along with General Butterfield's corps and Whipple's division, of Stoneman's Corps. On the left, Franklin's division crossed, along with Birney's and Sickle's divisions. At 11:00 a.m., Cowan returned to camp for repairs. He asked General Henry Jackson Hunt's headquarters to send new axles for his guns, but Hunt was not in his tent; he was at the front. Cowan returned to his camp, and decided to try to fix the guns himself. At 6:00 p.m., he returned with all six of his pieces ready for action.[liii]

At 8:00 a.m. the next morning, Cowan moved to Pollock's Mill and took a position a half mile to the left of the mill. Cowan joined Wever, Taft and Rickett's batteries. The batteries shelled the opposite woods, which sheltered the Rebel cavalry. The batteries drove the Rebel cavalry from the woods. When the Union skirmishers advanced, and the line of battle was formed to the front of Cowan's battery, he limbered up and moved one hundred yards to the rear. The Confederate shells reached their position but failed to do any damage. At dark, Cowan returned to camp and at 6:00 a.m. Sunday, took position on the extreme left of the Union line, and kept up a fire on any considerable body of rebel infantry that came into sight. He remained in his position and performed the same duty the next day. At 10:00 p.m. his men remained at their posts.[liv]

While Cowan's battery fired at Rebel cavalry, General Burnside formed his men to attack Marye's Heights. The left side of General Lee's line was anchored on Marye's Heights. Located on Marye's Heights was a 1,200 foot long stone wall. The retaining wall was built alongside the main road to Richmond and the troops behind the wall belonged to Confederate General Lafayette McClaws brigade, commanded by General Thomas R. R. Cobb. The Rebels were packed two ranks deep behind the wall and had a clear field of fire to their front. Around noon, Burnside's brigade marched out of Fredericksburg and charged the stone wall. Confederate artillery under Colonel E. Porter Alexander, located on Marye's Heights and the troops under Cobb opened fire on the oncoming Federal troops. The brigade fell and two more brigades charged with the same result. General Joseph Kershaw's brigade joined McLaw's brigade, making the Rebel line four men deep behind the wall. Burnside sent wave after wave of his infantry into the Confederate grinder. Darkness brought an end to the battle. Seven Union divisions charged fourteen times against Marye's Heights, but no Union soldier reached the wall. The closest any of the Union soldiers made to the wall was to within fifty yards. Burnside lost seven thousand men. Confederate losses were 1,200 men.[lv]

Burnside called for another attack for the next day, but his commanders convinced him that another attack would be futile and he revoked his order. Confederate General Thomas Jackson also called for a Confederate counterattack for the next day, but Confederate General Robert E. Lee opposed an attack, stating that Union artillery across the river dominated the open ground and his men would be enfiladed with cannon fire. Union causalities mounted to 12,653 killed, wounded and missing. Confederate losses were only 5,309 men. On December 15, the Union army re-crossed the river. Burnside had been defeated.[lvi]

During the engagement at Fredericksburg, Cowan fired 319 rounds. He did not lose any men or horses.[lvii] Captain Gustavus A. De Russy, Fourth U.S. Artillery, commanding the batteries on the left of the Union line, wrote in his official report of the battle about the "energy and vigilance displayed by Captain Cowan, First New York Battery. His practice was very annoying to the enemy, and the subject of admiration, commanding his battery with great judgment, and accomplishing the best results." [lviii]

Chapter 5

The Chancellorsville Campaign

After the disaster at Fredericksburg, President Abraham Lincoln relieved General Ambrose Burnside of command. On January 25, 1863, President Lincoln appointed General Joseph Hooker to command the Army of the Potomac. Hooker had 135,000 men and General Robert E. Lee had 60,000 men at Fredericksburg. Cowan's battery was under the VI Corps, under the command of General John Sedgwick, 2nd Division, under General Albion Howe. The division comprised of the 2nd Brigade, under the command of Colonel Lewis Grant, and the 3rd Brigade, under the command of General Thomas Neill. The Chief of Artillery was Colonel Charles Thompkins. The Artillery Brigade was under the command of Major J. Watts dePeyster, Jr.

The Artillery Brigade comprised of Cowan's battery and the 5th United States Battery F, under Lt. Leonard Martin. Hooker devised a strategy to defeat Lee. Hooker would leave a large force across the river from Lee and send one third of his army on a rapid march twenty miles up the Rappahannock River to cross at Kelley's Ford. The Union force would attack Lee's left and rear. Major General John Sedgwick, with another third of the army, would make a diversionary attack across the Rappahannock at Fredericksburg, keeping the Confederate soldiers in their works. The remaining third of the army would act as a reserve. Between April 27 and April 30, 75,000 Union soldiers made their crossing and passed through the undergrowth of the Wilderness, just ten miles from Fredericksburg. At noon, the different corps began arriving at a fifty acre clearing at a crossroads where the Chancellor House stood. Sedgwick's forty thousand-man force threatened the Confederate works at Fredericksburg. General Lee devised a plan where he would divide his army, leaving fourteen thousand men at Fredericksburg and sending Confederate General

Stonewall Jackson's twenty-six thousand men on the flank march. Lee would face Hooker's 75,000 men at Fredericksburg.[lix]

On May 1, Confederate General Stonewall Jackson's II Corps marched toward Chancellorsville. Union General Hooker's forces were marching out of the Wilderness into the open field. Jackson and Hooker's forces collided and a fierce fight took place. Hooker decided to fall back and formed a six-mile-long U shaped defensive position in the Wilderness.[lx]

Confederate General Lee realized that Hooker's withdrawal back into the Wilderness allowed the Confederates to fight on equal ground. The dense undergrowth of the Wilderness slowed Union movements and prevented the Union artillery from having a clear field of fire. During the night, Confederate cavalry General J.E.B. Stuart rode into Lee's camp and informed him that Hooker's right was unprotected. Lee decided to attack the vulnerable position.[lxi]

On May 2, Lee decided to divide his force again by sending Jackson's twenty-eight thousand men to march beyond the Union flank. At 5:30 p.m., Union General Oliver O. Howard's XI Corps was in their camps cooking dinner. At 6:00 p.m. Jackson's men attacked the completely surprised men of the XI Corps. The attack pushed back Hooker's flank for two miles. In the darkness, Jackson rode beyond his lines to reconnoiter for another attack. As he returned to his lines, he was shot by one of his own men who mistook Jackson for Union cavalry. Surgeons amputated Jackson's left arm, and then he contracted pneumonia, which ended the general's life on May 10.[lxii]

On May 3, Confederate General J.E.B. Stuart replaced Jackson and he resumed the attack. Stuart sent forward his men along a one and a quarter mile front. The attack ran over the first line of Union defenses and then stalled at the second line. From the high ground, at Hazel Grove, Confederate cannons, numbering around eighty guns, fired into the Union flank. Stuart attacked with a second wave of men, but the Confederates were brought to a halt. Stuart sent in a third and final line of men into the attack. The final wave managed to push the Union troops out of their entrenchments and sent them fleeing back to Chancellorsville. During the attack, Hooker was leaning on a column on the Chancellorsville house when a shell struck the column, stunning General Hooker. The fighting around Chancellorsville came to an end.[lxiii]

While Stuart attacked Hooker, Union General Sedgwick advanced toward Fredericksburg. Captain Cowan's battery was under the Sixth Army Corps, Second Division, under the command of Union General Albion P. Howe. At 11:00 a.m., May 3, the Sixth Corps prepared to attack the Rebels position between Hazel Run and Fredericksburg. Howe formed three columns. The first column was under General Thomas Neill and was comprised of the 7th Maine, the 79th New York, the 33rd New York, and a portion of the 21st New Jersey. The second column was under the command of Colonel Lewis Grant, and was comprised of the 2nd Vermont, the 6th Vermont, and the 26th New Jersey. The third column was comprised of the 3rd Vermont, the 4th Vermont, and a portion of the 21st New Jersey, led by Colonel Thomas Seaver. All three columns moved out. Howe placed his divisional artillery, including Cowan's battery, on a favorable range, where the guns could have an effective fire on the Confederate works, and allowing the Union line to advance without inferring with the artillery fire. Cowan took a position on the left of Fredericksburg, and shelled the Confederate's batteries on the heights. Howe order General Neil and Colonel Grant to charge with bayonets on Cemetery Hill. During the charge, Cowan kept up a rapid fire on all the Confederate works. After charging up Cemetery Hill, the Union assault was to turn on the main works on Marye's Hill. Howe ordered his divisional artillery, including Cowan's guns, to fire on the Confederate works on the heights and advanced the column, led by Colonel Seaver, to assault the same work. Cowan's battery succeeded in driving the Confederates from their works on the left, compelling them to abandon their pieces. Neil's column charged and carried the first work on Marye's Heights to Hazel Run and continued to the right and rear of the work. Grant's assault was on the Union right and front, while Seaver's attack was on the Union left. Each column charged and carried the first set of earthworks, and then three other works on the heights, taking two Rebel flags, all of the armaments of the works except one section of field artillery, some two hundred prisoners, and all of the Confederates camp equipment. A shell from Cowan's third piece exploded a Confederate limber in the right work carried by Howe's division. Howe commended Captain Cowan and Captain Martin's batteries for their "skill and efficiency with which they worked their batteries. The severe and well directed fire which they poured upon the enemy's works very materially impaired the force of the enemy's fire upon our storming columns." [lxiv]

After the attack, Howe was ordered to move his division on the Chancellorsville Road and join the other divisions of the corps. The advance of the corps encountered Confederate soldiers and his division broke out into a fight. Howe was ordered to throw his division to the left to stop a flank attack. At 3:00 p.m., Cowan received orders to follow the Third Brigade. They marched over the heights in the back of Fredericksburg, and followed in rear of the leading regiment of the Second Brigade, marching on the Plank Road leading to Culpepper Courthouse. He unlimbered on the left of the road. When no flank attack occurred, Howe decided to camp his division on the road. At 9:15 p.m. Cowan received orders to proceed to the front and came into battery on the right of the road near the toll gate. The Confederate skirmish line was in the edge of the woods, about seven hundred yards to Cowan's front.[lxv]

On May 4, Cowan discovered the Rebels building an earthwork in his front, using the planks from the road to strengthen the works. He directed a few well-directed shells to put a stop to the Confederate operations. During the day, the Confederates threatened his position several times, but did not attempt to advance in strong force.[lxvi]

At 5:00 p.m., the fighting broke out along the whole line, and attacked Howe's left and center, followed by a heavy column of infantry on his left. The Confederate attack on Howe's left was successfully broken and his right was advancing. Howe managed to capture twenty-one officers and nearly all the men from the Eighth Louisiana Regiment. Howe took a portion of his force on his right and reinforced his left and sent to headquarters asking for more additional men. On Howe's left, the Confederate forces were vigorously attacking the Union soldiers. Two Union regiments arrived to support Howe. The Confederates rallied and advanced until they brought their flank opposite the woods in which the Vermont brigade was placed. The Vermont brigade opened fire on the Confederate flank and the batteries opened fire. At 10:30 p.m., Howe moved his division to Bank's Ford and re-crossed the Rappahannock.[lxvii]

At 6:45 p.m., General John Sedgwick informed Cowan that he was about to withdraw the infantry, and ordered Cowan to hold his position as along as possible, holding on until General William Brooks passed. Lieutenant William Harn's battery was on Cowan's left, and a regiment was three hundred yards to his front. Cowan continued to fire on the Rebels until 7:30 p.m. Due to the withdrawal of Brooks's division and Harns's battery, as well as the rebel skirmishers advancing on Cowan's left and rear, he considered the time was right to withdraw. He fired by piece, starting on the right. As he fired each piece, the previously fired piece would limber up and move off the field, until the entire battery had vacated the field and moved to Bank's Ford. On arriving at the ford, his battery waited for four hours, waiting for orders to cross. While waiting to cross, Rebel shells exploded on or near the bridge every few minutes. At 1:00 a.m. Cowan was ordered to cross the bridge over the Rappahannock River and just as he began his crossing, two Confederate shells exploded on the middle of the bridge where two minutes before the battery had just passed.[lxviii] Cowan did not lose a single man during the crossing. During the Chancellorsville campaign, Cowan's battery fired 545 rounds.[lxix]

Confederate General Lee managed to stop Sedgwick's advance, and two days later, Hooker retreated across the Rappahannock River. The Chancellorsville Campaign was Lee's masterpiece. Lee managed to recover the initiative, and executed a flawless offensive. Hooker should have never abandoned his advance at Chancellorsville. Hooker let 75,000 Union soldiers sit idle all day, more than deploying them into the fight. The Confederate victory resulted in the loss of 12,764 Confederate soldiers from his sixty thousand soldiers, while Hooker lost 17,287 out of his 130,000 Union soldiers. Lee suffered heavy losses, including the loss of Confederate General Stonewall Jackson, but his victory over a superior Union army convinced him that his soldiers, if properly led, were invincible.[lxx]

Chapter 6

The Battle of Gettysburg

In May of 1863, President Jefferson Davis, his cabinet members and his generals met to discuss his options for the next move against the Union troops. Union General Ulysses S. Grant laid siege on Vicksburg, Mississippi, but Confederate General Robert E. Lee advised Davis not to reinforce Vicksburg and invade Tennessee, but suggested another invasion of the North. Lee told Davis that an invasion of the North would relieve Richmond from Federal pressure, help gather badly needed supplies from the Pennsylvania countryside, encourage the Northern peace movement, and reopen the possibility for European support.[lxxi]

On June 3, Confederate General Lee pulled out most of his reorganized army from Fredericksburg with only Major General Ambrose P. Hill's III Corps remaining in the town. By June 8, Lee concentrated two infantry corps and his cavalry at Culpepper. Two days later General Richard Ewell's II Corps moved toward the Shenandoah Valley. By June 13, Ewell reached Winchester. Ewell attacked Union General Robert Milroy's Union force and destroyed his command. With the lower valley clear of Union troops, Lee's Army of Northern Virginia crossed the Potomac River into Maryland. By June 25, Confederate troops entered Northern territory.[lxxii]

Once Hooker was informed of the Confederate invasion of the North, he marched north. After arguing with General Henry Halleck over the garrison at Harpers Ferry, Hooker resigned. Lincoln accepted the resignation and appointed General George Meade to command the army. When Lee learned of Meade's position, he gathered his infantry units, which were scattered across Pennsylvania. Advance units of General Lee's army arrived at Harrisburg. Lee ordered his army to converge on Cashtown.[lxxiii]

On June 28, 1863, the VI Corps, under the command of General John Sedgwick, 3rd Division, under the command of General John

Newton and General Frank Wheaton, along with the Artillery Brigade, under the command of Colonel Charles Thompkins, including Captain Andrew Cowan, marched from Edwards Ferry, Maryland, to Hyattstown.

Colonel Charles Tompkins was born on May 15, 1834. He was the son of John and Anna Tompkins of New Windsor. In 1844, the family moved to Rhode Island. He received his education from the public schools in Rhode Island and when he graduated from high school, he entered into the mercantile profession. At the outbreak of the Civil War, he was in command of the Marine Corps of Artillery, which was activated in 1853. The Marine Artillery was the first to volunteer for three months service. On April 17, 1861, the Marine Artillery left Providence, Rhode Island and fell under the command of General Patterson. In August of 1861, Tompkins was promoted to the rank of major and on September 13, he was given the command of the 1st Rhode Island Light Artillery. In November of 1861, he was assigned duty as chief of artillery to Brigadier General Stone. He served as chief of artillery throughout the Peninsular Campaign. He received reports from his superior officers for his meritorious and gallant conduct for his actions at Fair Oaks, Savage Station, Glendale, and Malvern Hill.[lxxiv]

On June 30, 1863, Cowan's artillery arrived at Manchester. While in Manchester, the officers of the First New York Independent Battery were invited to a reception and buffet supper which Union ladies were to give that night in honor of the Union officers guarding the town. Cowan rode in after dark, accompanied by Lieutenant Johnson, leaving orders with Lieutenant Wright to send a courier after them if any order to move was received. Cowan and his officers were late to the reception, but in time for the supper. The doors between the parlor and dining room were opened, revealing a long table loaded with Maryland fried chicken and other delicacies, also great dishes of fruit and an array of bottles. A charming lady took Cowan's arm and as they stood at the table waiting to be served, one of Cowan's buglers ran in, bringing a message from General Wright that the battery was already breaking camp. Cowan had not heard the lady's name but as he turned to rush from the room, she reached for one of the bottles, saying "Take this, Captain." Cowan thrust the bottle into one of his saddle pockets, buckled the flap over it, and rode away to overtake the leading brigade of the Union Third Division and arrived at Rock Creek crossing on the

Baltimore road to Gettysburg at 1:00 p.m. after continuous marching day and night.[lxxv]

On July 1, a Confederate infantry brigade under Confederate General Henry Heth, marching east on the Chambersburg Pike in search of shoes, clashed with two Union cavalry brigades under Union General John Buford, just west of Gettysburg. Buford knew the importance of Gettysburg, where nine roads converged. He deployed his men to confront the oncoming Confederates. At 8:00 a.m., Heth charged the discounted cavalry, who were armed with Spencer repeating carbines. The Federals repulsed several Confederate attacks. At 10:30 a.m., Union General John Reynold's I Corps relieved Buford's command. After Confederate General Ambrose Hill ordered Heth to attack, Heth and General William Pender's division charged into Reynold's lines on McPherson's Ridge. During the battle, Reynold's was killed by a Confederate sharpshooter's bullet. The Confederates seized the ridge, pushing the Yankees back to Seminary Ridge. Shortly after noon, Union General Oliver Howard's XI Corps reached the field, deploying north of Gettysburg. Two of Ewell's Confederate divisions arrived on the field. Ewell charged Howard's men and pushed back his men with heavy losses. Howard's men fled through the town. Hill renewed his attacks and the Union I Corps also fled after being attacked from the front and rear. While the I Corps and XI corps was being pushed back through town, Union General Winfield Hancock arrived on Cemetery Hill and rallied the fleeing Union troops. Lee ordered Ewell to attack Hancock, but Ewell never attacked Hancock's position.[lxxvi]

At 9:00 p.m., Sedgwick ordered the VI Corps to move out and march to Gettysburg. Cowan harnessed up his six three-inch ordnance rifles and followed the leading brigade of the Third Division of the VI Corps. As the hot sun arose in the morning, Cowan's battery rested and began to make breakfast. Just as they were preparing their morning meal, orders were issued to march out. By 9:00 a.m., as Cowan approached Gettysburg, he could hear the thunder of cannons and by 10:00 a.m., Cowan's battery crossed into Pennsylvania. By noon, Cowan could see the burst of artillery shells in the air. Captain Cowan's artillery arrived near the field of Gettysburg.[lxxvii]

On July 2, the Union forces manned a strong defensive position south and east of Gettysburg. Resembling a giant fishhook, the line stretched from Culp's Hill to Cemetery Hill, along Cemetery Ridge to the base of Little Round Top. The southern area, Little Round Top and Big Round Top were undefended. By 1:00 p.m., Cowan's battery arrived at the bridge over Rock Creek when his battery moved out of the road into the fields at their left, but the infantry pushed on to the vicinity of Little Round Top, near the position held by the 3rd Corps.[lxxviii] Two Confederate divisions commanded by Generals John Bell Hood and Lafayette McLaws from General James Longstreet's corps attacked and overran the advanced position held by the III Corps, pushing them men back up Cemetery Ridge. At 6:20 p.m., Confederate General Richard Anderson, from General Ambrose Hill's Corps, sent his division forward in an attack on Union line at Cemetery Hill just left of Longstreet's men. General Cadmus Wilcox's brigade attacked first, followed by Colonel David Lang's brigade and finally General Ambrose Wright's brigade. The Confederates drove the Union troops up the slopes of Cemetery Ridge. Union General Winfield Hancock took most of the men out of his line to reinforce the left and the Confederates soldiers charged straight into the Union gap. Hancock called for reinforcements, and sent the 1st Minnesota to charge the oncoming Confederates. Four-fifths of the 1st Minnesota fell in the charge. During the charge, Hancock managed to fill the gap with more reinforcements into the Confederate lines. The Confederates kept coming up the slope and pushed through the Union lines and up to the crest of the hill, but without support, the Union troops attacked from both sides, and the Rebels had no choice but to fall back. The fight on Cemetery Ridge came to an end.[lxxix]

Meanwhile General Richard Ewell's II Corps moved towards the far right of the Union line in order to keep the Union troops in placed and prevent them from reinforcing their left, where the main Rebel attack would occur. At 5:00 p.m., the Rebel batteries opened fire against Cemetery Hill and Culp's Hill. When Ewell attacked he found little resistance from the Union troops. As night fell, the two brigades assaulting Culp's Hill struggled up the steep wooded slope and through abandoned Union rifle pits, because the 12th Corps was ordered away from the rifle pits to the support of the Union left wing.[lxxx] The Union troops put up a strong Union defense and the Confederate soldiers were not able to break through the Union lines. Darkness ended the fight and both sides slept on their firearms. The two brigades that charged up Cemetery Hill routed the Union XI Corps, capturing two batteries, and managed to arrive on the crest of the Hill. Union reinforcements arrived, and the Rebel troops were pushed back to the base of the hill. Darkness ended the fighting.[lxxxi]

Cowan's battery's right was on the Baltimore Pike, commanding the open area to the west. All of the batteries of the artillery brigade of the 6th Corps were placed in position along the high ground overlooking the valley of Rock Creek and the road to Gettysburg, prepared to sweep the flank of Confederate General Edward Johnson's division if they planned to move forward to the turnpike of the rear of the Union right center along Cemetery Ridge.[lxxxii]

During the night, Colonel Charles Tompkins, the commander of the artillery brigade, ordered Cowan and his men at their posts all night and to be constantly on the alert. Soon after daylight, Cowan was ordered to report to General John Newton, commanding the First Corps. Cowan marched across the bridge and up the Baltimore road, to the first road turning to his left, which the staff officer led Cowan to the Taneytown road in rear of the northern edge of Little Round Top. Cowan reached the front at 10:00 a.m., but General Newton was not in camp. He moved his battery forward and reported to General Abner Doubleday, who decided that no more batteries were required and told Cowan to park nearby. Doubleday told Cowan: "Come with me Captain, and I will show the situation." [lxxxiii] Cowan rode through the grove to the west side, the general walking beside Cowan's horse. Captain Cowan saw the Union troops behind a strong rifle pit which extended a long distance to the right and left. Over beyond them, near the Emmittsburg Road, he could plainly see the Confederates placing a battery of brass guns. The General said to Cowan: "You can see that if I should put your battery in now, it would draw fire of all the guns along yonder ridge, and would cause us to lose many men without doing any good. Park your battery at some convenient place, let your men get their breakfast, send me word where you are, and when I can use you I will send for you." [lxxxiv] Cowan's battery pulled off into a field. In the field was a grove of trees, which his men welcomed the shade from the hot July sun. The men began to make coffee.

After some time had passed, Cowan rode back to inspect the line of battle, followed by his bugler, Lt. Lewis Tallman. He rode to the north to some scrub oaks known as the "corpse of trees," on Cemetery Ridge. The right of Doubleday's division did not extend that far north. To the left of the tress for a distance, the line was held by Colonel Norman Hall's and General William Harrow's brigades of General John Gibbon's division of the 2nd Corps. After getting the best possible view of the Confederate guns, which were covering a commanding ridge along the Emmittsburg road, and estimating the distance for his guns, Cowan road back to the battery.[lxxxv]

Little did Cowan know that Confederate General Robert E. Lee planned to assault Cemetery Ridge. Lee would send eleven brigades, under the command of General George Pickett to assault Cemetery Ridge, while General J.E.B. Stuart would assault the Union rear from the east with his cavalry. The Confederate I Corps, under the command of General James Longstreet, ordered into line General George Pickett's three brigades of Virginians, followed by General James Johnston Pettigrew's four brigades, on Pickett's left, and in Pettigrew's rear was General Isaac R. Tremble's two brigades. Advancing in support of the nine Confederate brigades was General Richard Anderson's Alabama brigade, and a small Florida brigade. The Confederate soldiers were to advance over a mile of open ground. Before the Confederate infantry started their attack, Colonel E.P. Alexander, chief of artillery for the Army of Northern Virginia, would fire his one hundred and forty cannons at the Union position on Cemetery Ridge.[lxxxvi]

Just before 8:00 a.m., Cowan dismounted his horse, unbuckled his overcoat from his saddle. He gave his reins of his horse to his bugler, who was to lead his horse down to the left. He laid his coat on the ground and was dropping down to get some rest when a shell flew screaming over their heads towards the clump of trees, followed by another, and then a third Confederate shell went flying over their heads. The three shells hit the limbers in Lieutenant Alonzo H. Cushing's Battery A, 4th United States Artillery. Huge explosions erupted. After the explosions, Union troops removed the flaming limber chests. Soon, the entire woods were tumbling down on Cowan's men. The air filled with shot and bursting shell around Cemetery Ridge. The Confederate guns aimed too high, so that the limbs of the trees far over their heads suffered most of the damage. Many of Cowan's men scattered "like partridges" at the first outburst of artillery fire and the deluge of falling limbs from the tree tops.[lxxxvii]

Cowan jumped up from the ground, shouted for the bugler to bring his horse and threw on his coat over the rear ammunition chest of the nearest caisson and turned to grasp the reins of his horse just as his bugler's horse was killed under him. The bugler signaled "Stand to Horse," "Cannoneers to your Post!" Cowan moved out into the road again and halted in column at the junction with the Taneytown Road. Cowan met Lieutenant Colonel Warner, of the artillery, with orders to put them in position on the front line near the extreme right of General Abner Doubleday's division.[lxxxviii]

Before passing through the grove of trees beyond the First Corps Headquarters, Cowan ordered his caissons to remain there in the pasture field, where they would be within easy call and less exposed to shells, which might explode their full chests of ammunition. When cleared of the trees, Cowan turned to the right, until Colonel Edward Warner pointed out a position for their guns.[lxxxix]

Cowan opened fire at once, directing his aim to the left oblique. He fired very slowly and methodically. Cowan was taught by his former commander General Romeyn Ayres, who fought with Cowan through the Peninsular Campaign and Antietam, to make sure every one of his shots counted and never get excited.[xc]

On Cowan's right was Battery B, 1st New York Regiment of Artillery, under the command of Captain James Rorty. He had fired forty-five rounds of shell and shrapnel that was in his six gun limbers, and the caisson limbers were coming up with full chests to take their place when a staff officer, riding at full speed from his right, shouted: "Cease firing! Hold your fire for the infantry." Cowan ceased fire but could not see anything in front of them because of the thick smoke.[xci]

After the smoke cleared, another officer shouted from his horse as he rode to the left, and told Cowan to report to General Alexander Webb on his right. Webb belonged to the 2nd Corps. Looking to his right, Cowan saw an officer standing near the clump of trees, waving his hat at Cowan and he saw that a battery at the left of the trees was withdrawing their guns. The officer was General Webb, and the battery was Captain Thomas Brown's 1st Rhode Island, which was disabled and out of ammunition and their officer, Captain Brown, was wounded.[xcii] The 1st Rhode Island lost twenty-two men and thirty horses. The dead horses were piled around the low hill in front of the Cemetery Ridge defense lines.[xciii]

Cowan gave the order to "Limber to the right" and the battery raced forward to the trees at a gallop. The artillery duel between the Confederate batteries and the Union batteries continued for two hours. Several of Cowan's men had taken off their coats and vests, because of the blazing July hot sun. The Confederate cannons stopped firing and just before 3:00 p.m., eleven thousand Confederate soldiers emerged from Seminary Ridge. Pickett's advance against Meade's position at Cemetery Ridge began. Once in Cowan's new position, he saw beyond the Emmittsburg Road what the order was meant by holding his fire for the infantry. Cowan saw the gleaming bayonets of Pickett, Pettigrew, Tremble and Anderson's eleven brigades. He could see their battle flags waving as their lines moved forward.[xciv]

Rorty's New York Battery, on Cowan's right, and Alonzo Cushing's regular battery, also on Cowan's right, with the clump of trees between them, were firing rapidly at the oncoming brigades. Gaps opened in the Confederate lines as the Union batteries fired canister and shell. The Confederates closed their gaps and kept advancing. Cowan opened fire with his battery, but noticed that only five of his six guns were in position at the left of the trees. The leading gun, when coming up at a gallop, passed to the right of the trees and Cowan found the gun, under the command of Corporal Mullaly. The gun moved into position but was too close to Cushing's cannons and could not be worked. Lt. Alonzo Cushing road up and he made some pleasant reply to Cowan's hurried explanation. Cushing turned around and shouted the order: "By hand to the front," meaning that his left guns would be pushed forward, making room for Cowan's gun, under Corporal Mullaly. Cowan watched as Cushing's men pulled their left gun by hand to the wall. A stone wall ran south along Cemetery Ridge from the front of Ziegler's Grove, then turned at right angles a couple hundred yards apart, north of the corpse of trees, then ran west about a hundred feet, and again turned to the south, passing the western edge of the trees and continuing onto connecting with rifle pits.[xcv]

General Alexander Webb's Brigade held the wall inside the angle, with their left extending south of the trees and for about fifty yards. The brigade comprised of the 69th, 71st, 72nd, and 106th Pennsylvania, with three to four hundred men in each regiment. The first three regiments positioned themselves behind the wall looking west, while the remaining two companies of the 106th Pennsylvania were located behind the wall facing north. The remainder of the 106th Pennsylvania was on detached duty, but arrived in time for the battle. At the right angle was Captain William Arnold's Rhode Island Battery with General William Hay's division, which held the stone wall to Ziegler's Grove and beyond. Lieutenant George Woodruff's 1st U. S. Battery I was further to the right of the angle than Arnold's. Cushing's 4th U. S. Battery A was placed in the angle at the right of the trees, along the ridge about online with the eastern edge of the clump of trees. Cowan's battery, which replaced Brown's battery, had one gun on the right of the trees and the other five guns to the left of them, on the same line as Cushing's held. Two or three companies of the 69th regiment, the left regiment of Webb's brigade, were at the wall directly in front of Cowan's guns. To the left of the Cowan's battery was Battery B, 1st New York, under the command of Captain James Rorty. In their front were Colonel Norman Hall's and General William Harrow's brigades of General John Gibbon's division of the 2nd Corps.[xcvi]

Every gun from Cemetery Ridge to the Round Top was firing on the oncoming Confederates, with their front extending far to the right and left of the angle as they advanced. Cowan could see the Confederates advancing to the Emmittsburg Road. Cowan poured shell and shrapnel into the Rebel lines.[xcvii] Confederate General George Pickett's three brigades were heading straight for Cowan's guns.

General Henry Hunt, chief of artillery, rode into Cowan's battery. Cowan stood by his horses and saw him begin firing at the Confederates with his revolver, shouting: "See'em, See'em, See'em." Then his horse was killed out from under him. Cowan gave Sergeant Van Etten's horse to the general. As the general rode away, he shouted: "Look out, or you will kill your men," meaning the 69th Pennsylvania Infantry at the wall. That was the only order given to Cowan during the battle. Cowan ordered his men to load double canister to be ready should the Confederates take the front wall.[xcviii]

As the Confederate soldiers approached the stone wall, a large number of Pickett's men, under the command of General James Kemper' brigade, lay down among the dead battery horses of Cushing's battery. The Confederates began to fire rounds into Cowan's artillery. To the left of Cowan's guns, the brigades under General Lewis Armstead and Richard Garnett overran Cushing's guns, which seized firing. Lieutenant Cushing was dead, shot through the mouth by a bullet. *(Note: one hundred and fifty years later, on November 6, 2014, President Obama awarded Cushing the Congressional Medal of Honor for his actions that day.)*

Suddenly, the men of the 69th Pennsylvania and 59th New York, at the wall in their front, jumped up and ran through the tress to the right. Cowan saw one of the infantry officers running "like turkey, with his sword tucked under his arm, and his face distorted with fear." Corporal Plunkett of Cowan's battery watched as the infantrymen ran past his cannon and swore at them "like a pirate." He picked up a large coffee pot by the handle, and smashed pot over the head of one of the frightened soldiers. Cowan stated that the "bottom [of the pot] broke in, but that fellow went on running with the tin pot down on his ears."[xcix]

Cowan's front was now exposed, and a large number of Confederates under the 9th and 14th Virginia, lay down behind a slight elevation about two hundred yards in Cowan's front, which was covered with bushes and rocks. Cowan ordered his cannons to fire double canister. As he yelled his command to "Fire," Lieutenant William Wright, standing alongside him, was badly wounded. Wright made the third officer lost during the battle. During the battle, Lieutenant Theodore Atkins was taken to the rear from sunstroke and Lieutenant William Johnson had also been wounded. James McElroy, attending the cannon nearest the clump of trees called out to Cowan: "Captain, this is out last round." He rammed the canister into the barrel, stepped beside the right wheel, and fell, his face pierced by three bullets."[c]

Just as Cowan loaded his last round of canister into his five guns, the soldiers of the 9th and 14th Virginia leaped up and rushed towards Cowan's position, with the intent of taking his guns.[ci] A Confederate major began yelling, and he was followed by a number of Confederate soldiers. The soldiers began to cross the wall and Cowan heard the major shout: "Take the guns!" Cowan ordered double canister at twenty yards and yelled: "Fire!" hurling two hundred and twenty round balls of lead from each of the five guns into the charging Confederates. The canister fire literally swept the Confederates from Cowan's front. Later, after the battle was over, Cowan walked to the fallen Confederates and found the Confederate major's body and sword. Cowan buried the Confederate officer with honors and returned the sword twenty-five years later to some of Pickett's veterans.[cii]

Cowan was pulling his guns back when he saw that the Confederates were running and that large numbers were throwing down their arms. At the right of the trees, Confederate General Louis Armistead had broken through the Union lines, with a number of his men. Cowan saw the Union colors of several regiments back on a line with him, about where Cushing's guns were located and one of Cowan's guns had been surrounded by masses of Union soldiers who were firing as fast as they could load.[ciii]

Pickett's men charged the Union line and desperate hand to hand combat broke out, but there were not enough Confederates left after the charge to hold onto wall. The Confederates only choice was to surrender or to go back across the mile of open ground. Pickett's division was almost annihilated and those who had not fallen or surrendered were in full retreat. Almost four thousand Confederate soldiers were captured. General Pickett lost seventy percent of his division. Union losses amounted to only 1,500 men, only one fifth of the number engaged in the battle.[civ]

As the Confederates retreated from Pickett's failed charge, the Union artillerists from ten cannons on Cowan's right and the batteries on Cowan's left had retired. Confederate Colonel E. P. Alexander advanced several smooth bore batteries to within 1,300 yards of Cowan's position on the Emmittsburg Road in order to cover the retreat or prevent pursuit. The Confederate cannons opened fire on part of the line Cowan occupied. Cowan concentrated his fire on a single battery. Sergeant Van Etten aimed one of the two guns they had in working order and exploded four of the Confederate limbers in rapid succession. Cowan flung his coat on the ground and aimed the other gun. After a few shots, the Confederate battery limbered up and rode off. Another three-inch battery rode up on Cowan's left and opened fire. After about an hour, there was only one section of Confederate artillery firing and the section soon limbered up and rode off. As the section of artillery was galloping off, a shell from Cowan's battery from his right cannon exploded one of the Rebel limbers. Once the Confederate section of guns rode off, the fighting ended for Cowan's men.[cv]

Cowan's men suffered from extreme thirst, and none of the men had a canteen of water. Cowan remembered the bottle of claret wine in his saddle bags. Cowan had to strip the harness from his dead horses, rearrange the gun detachments and put the battery in serviceable condition even before he could aid the wounded. General Webb gave Cowan a detail of ten men from the 20th Massachusetts Infantry to assist Cowan.[cvi]

Cowan's coat was stolen when he threw the coat aside and he was in shirtsleeves, but he walked down to the wall and over it. On the Union side of the wall were both the bodies of blue and grey soldiers, while beyond the wall the ground was thickly covered with dead and wounded Virginians. Cowan stated that the scene was "a pitiful spectacle and the cries of the wounded were agonizing."[cvii]

After the Pickett's charge, Cowan rode to the house at Taneytown Road where he found Lieutenant Wright, who was shot through the lungs, and Private Gates, who had both legs broken, lying on the ground in the little orchard. Cowan gave both men a drink of his claret wine, and gave each of the other wounded men closest to his wounded men, a sip from the bottle until the bottle was completely empty.[cviii]

Cowan took possession of a bedroom on the ground floor of a farm house behind the round top, and had Lieutenant Wright and Lieutenant Johnson from his command carried to the house. Wright had the big family bed and Johnson had a cot on the opposite side of the room. Just then a Confederate officer from North Carolina who had been wounded at the front wall held by Hay's division of the Second Corps, whose arm had been amputated, was carried into the hall on a stretcher. Cowan had another cot brought into the room for the wounded Confederate.[cix]

After the failure of Pickett's charge, General Robert E. Lee realized that the only option he had was to retreat south toward Virginia. Lee decided to hold his position on Seminary Ridge while the wagon trains carrying more than ten thousand wounded men moved north, toward South Mountain to Chambersburg. The wagons would move south to Williamsport, Maryland. After the wagons were safe, the rest of the army would march south and reunite with the wounded at Williamsport. On July 4, at 4:00 p.m., General John Imboden, with 2,100 cavalrymen and twenty-three cannon, began escorting the seventeen mile-long wagon train of wounded from Seminary Ridge. Rain began to pour down from the skies all night and day turning the roads into mud.[cx]

On July 5, the wagons arrived at Williamsport, but the rain swollen river made the ford crossing of the wagons impossible. After dark on July 4, Lee's I and II Corps held their position on Seminary Ridge while the III Corps started the retreat. By July 5, the I, III, and the II Corps retreated from the battlefield. The Battle of Gettysburg was officially over. More than fifty thousand soldiers fell on the battlefield. Of the 82,000 Union soldiers engaged during the battle, 3,155 were killed, 14,529 wounded, and 5,365 missing. The 75,000 Confederates lost 3,903 killed, 18,735 wounded, and 5,425 missing. The Union victory at Gettysburg and the victory at Vicksburg was a turning point in the war.[cxi]

On July 5, Cowan's battery was relieved by Battery G, First Rhode Island Artillery, and returned to camp, but immediately marched with the Sixth Corps, in pursuit of the retreating Confederates. Cowan placed one section near Millerstown, Pennsylvania. Before Cowan left in pursuit of the Confederate, he rode over to the house to say good-bye to his officers. Lieutenant Wright was supported on his bed by two of Cowan's men, and seemed about to breathe his last. Cowan told him that he had sent a courier to Westminster the day before with a telegram message for his father and mother to come at once, and that they would surely arrive the following day. Cowan turned to Lieutenant Johnson, suffering from a severe flesh wound in his hip, and told him to keep his two men until Wright's father and mother arrived. Then Cowan walked to the side of the Confederate soldier and expressed his sympathy and assured him that he would be well cared for. He looked at Cowan gravely, without speaking word, but his eyes were overflowing as Cowan turned away. Lieutenant Wright's life was saved because he was young, strong and temperate and had the devoted care of his father and sister until he could be taken home. But his career as an artillery officer was ended. Lieutenant Johnson recovered and promptly returned to the battery, in which he later fell mortally wounded at Winchester. The field hospital of the First New Jersey Brigade was established around the house behind the round top. Cowan met the brigade surgeon twenty-three years later at Fredericksburg and asked him if he could tell Cowan anything about the wounded Confederate officer. The surgeon told Cowan that the captain was not doing well and the surgeon diagnosed his case as depression from mental worry. He asked him to speak to him as freely as though he were his family physician at home. The Confederate captain told the surgeon: "Doctor, I don't want the news of my being wounded to get out. My wife is about to become a mother and if she hears of my being shot it will kill her."[cxii] The Confederate captain had only been married to his wife less than a year and learned the news about his pregnant wife from a letter from home he received on the march to Gettysburg. The surgeon managed to keep the captain's name off the wounded list. The surgeon also wrote a letter for him and told the captain he had means for getting it to Richmond. The captain recovered, the letter had reached his wife and she was saved. Letters passed between the doctor and the soldier after the war. One day, about twenty years later, a young man entered the doctor's office, greeted him and said: "Doctor, I am up at Princeton College. You saved my father's life and my mother's and mine and my father told me to find you here and say: Doctor, I am the boy."[cxiii] Cowan's battery continued the pursuit of Lee's Army of Northern Virginia until July 25, when it was called off. Cowan's battery stopped their pursuit at Warrentown.[cxiv]

Chapter 7

The Mine Run Campaign

After the Battle of Gettysburg, General Robert E. Lee's 48,500 men of the Army of Northern Virginia set up a defensive line along the Rappahannock River. On November 26, Union General George Meade, of the Army of the Potomac, intended to attack Lee's right flank, which was the nearest and most exposed. Meade hoped to quickly deliver a crushing blow to the right flank before Lee could reinforce the exposed flank. Union General William H. French, commander of the leading Union corps, advanced slowly towards Lee's flank. French's slow march allowed Lee to bring up his III Corps while the II Corps, commanded by General Jubal Early, confronted the federal advance. On November 26, Cowan's battery marched with the artillery brigade in the direction of the Rapidan and on November 27, at 1:30 a.m., he crossed the river at Germanna. Fighting broke out between the Union Third Corps and Early's II Corps on at Payne's farm. Cowan joined the III Corps near the Morris farm, where the Third Corps was engaged in battle. Both armies lost more than five hundred men before the Confederates fell back at nightfall behind the valley of Mine Run, a stream that runs into the Rapidan. The Confederates dug in and waited for the arrival of the III Corps and hoped the Union troops would attack their entrenchments.[cxv]

On November 28, Cowan's battery marched with the brigade and joined the rest of the army near Robertson's Tavern. On November 29, Cowan erected earthworks and placed his guns in position on a crest a short distance to the right of the Orange Courthouse turnpike. At 8:00 a.m., on November 30, Cowan opened fire on the Confederates works, fired forty-six rounds, and received orders to cease fire.[cxvi]

Union General Gouverneur K. Warren had arrived below Lee's position and notified Meade that he thought he could turn the Confederate line. On November 29 and 30, Lee had extended and fortified his line, and Warren realized that a general assault would be useless. Meade called off the assault. On December 1, Cowan withdrew from his position, and on December 2, he re-crossed the Rapidan at Germanna. On December 2, Lee realized that the Federals did not intend to attack his position and decided to take the offensive. When he learned that Meade retreated, Lee exclaimed: "I am too old to command this army. We should never have permitted those people to get away."[cxvii] By December 3, 1863, Cowan's battery was positioned near Brandy Station, Virginia. In January 1864, Cowan secured permission to go on leave and he married his childhood sweetheart Mary Adsit. Just before his wedding, he re-enlisted, along with nearly all of the other men in his battery.[cxviii]

Chapter 8

The Rapidan and James River Campaign: The Overland Campaign

During the month of May, Union General Ulysses S. Grant started his Overland Campaign. Grant ordered Union General George Meade and his 120,000 men to cross the Rapidan River. Waiting for Meade, south of the river, was Confederate General Robert E. Lee's 60,000 men. From May 4, 1864 to June 12, both armies fought in some of the most vicious, bloody battles. During the Overland Campaign, Grant continually fought Lee, making the campaign a war of attrition.[cxix]

On May 4, 1864, Cowan's brigade along with the corps left their winter camp near Brandy Station and crossed the Rapidan River. Cowan marched with the Artillery Brigade from Germanna Ford to the Rapidan. The next day, the brigade moved with the corps on the Germanna Road to the intersection of plank road and Orange Courthouse and Fredericksburg Road, when the Confederate army met them in force. The Corps established a battle line and the artillery crossed in their rear.[cxx] Confederate General Richard Ewell's II Corps advanced on the Orange Turnpike. Ewell deployed two divisions bordering on the woods around Sander's Field. Union General Romeyn Ayres' brigade, led by the 140th New York, charged out of the woods. The Rebel fire stopped the 140th New York dead in their tracks. Ayres sent in three more regiments, but the Rebel fire sent most of the regiments running back to the woods. Only the 140th New York and the 146th New York remained on the battlefield. The two regiments were ordered to attack, but again the two regiments met destructive Confederate fire. Two unlimbered Union cannons advanced into the field, and managed to fire two rounds into the 140th and 146th New York. The friendly fire did not stop the two New York regiments in attacking the Rebel lines. On the other side of the turnpike, a Union brigade managed to break through the Rebel lines but without any support, the men had to fall back before the relentless Rebel fire. The Union attack came to an end. Each side built defensive positions. When the 140th and 146th New York charged into battle that day, they had 1,600 men, by the end of the battle they had only 567 men left.[cxxi]

On May 6, at 5:00 a.m., General Ulysses Grant planned a two-pronged attack. He would attack west down the Orange Plank Turnpike with five divisions and at the same time send Union General Winfield Hancock's nine divisions west down the paralleling Orange Plank Road and attack General A. P. Hill's III Corps. Twenty thousand Union soldiers in three lines moved forward through thick undergrowth at the Wilderness and attacked Lee's III Corps. Lee's army set up a defensive line across Orange Plank Road. The Union soldiers managed to push back the Confederate soldiers for a mile. Confederate General James Longstreet's I Corps arrived and formed his lines. Confederate General John Gregg of the Texas brigade attacked, but within ten minutes he lost half of his force. Longstreet sent in four more brigades and the Union troops were pushed back to where they originally started. The worn out soldiers stopped their attack and built new defensive positions.[cxxii]

Although Cowan missed the Battle of the Wilderness, his battery continued to march with the brigade to Chancellorsville, Wilderness Tavern and onto the Piney Branch Road. After the bloody two-day battle of the Wilderness, Lee thought that Grant might try and move around his right and try to get between his Army of Northern Virginia and Richmond. Lee began to pull his troops out of the Wilderness and marched them towards the road to Spotsylvania Courthouse. Lee hoped to slow down Grant's army by sending Confederate General Jeb Stuart's cavalry against Grant's columns and protecting Lee's route. Grant sent Union General Phil Sheridan's cavalry to cut off Lee's route and hold the crossroads. On May 7, Stuart and Sheridan collided at Todd's Tavern. The Confederate cavalry retired and the Union cavalry held the field. The battle continued the next day with heavy losses on both sides. The Confederate cavalry were pushed back to Spotsylvania. They were about the abandon the crossroads, when Confederate General Richard Anderson's corps of infantry arrived across a bridge that Sheridan was ordered to destroy. On May 8, the Confederates reached Spotsylvania first and secured the area.[cxxiii]

On May 9, Lee and Grant faced each other once again. Both armies strengthened and extended their lines. While Union forces were strengthening their lines, a Confederate sharpshooter killed Union General John Sedgwick. On that same day, Cowan received orders from Colonel Charles Thompkins, commander of the artillery brigade, to place his guns in battery at the front, on the left of Piney Branch Road. Captain McCartney's battery was on Cowan's right and the infantry of the First and Second Division were a short distance to his front. Cowan entrenched during the afternoon under a moderate fire from the rebel batteries. On May 10, Grant ordered several attacks, all of which were repulsed. At 8:00 a.m., the Confederate batteries fired on Cowan, so he opened fire in response and silenced the opposing guns. At 5:00 p.m., Cowan received orders to open a rapid fire for ten minutes when the Union infantry charged the rebel works. Cowan fired for an hour. At 6:10 p.m., Union Colonel Emory Upton led twelve Union regiments forward in a charge on a narrow front that carried the Rebel works, and spread out on the left and right. But the Union attack was unsupported by other Union troops before the Confederates regrouped, and with additional reinforcements, mounted a countercharge that pushed back the Union soldiers back to their original lines. Cowan resumed firing for a half hour to silence the rebel guns, which were firing on the Union infantry.[cxxiv]

On May 11, Captain George Adams's battery relieved Cowan's guns and he moved to the forks of the Piney Branch and Todd's Tavern, where he received orders to march two miles to the left. He returned to the Piney Branch and camped for the night. For three days, Lee's army dug entrenchments at the crossroads at Spotsylvania Courthouse. At Lee's center line was a V-shaped salient or protrusion in the line called the "Mule Shoe." Because of the vulnerability of the position, Lee's men built sharpened branches pointing out in front of the trench line built of logs and earth. A maze of trenches with piled dirt protected Lee's men while they moved around in the Mule Shoe. Although Grant's attack failed, he decided would attack again the next day. Grant moved his II Corps into position in order to attack the Mule Shoe. Mistakenly, Lee thought Grant was withdrawing his men to find another route to Richmond. Lee ordered most of his artillery in the Mule Shoe removed.[cxxv]

At 9:00 a.m. the next morning, Union General Winfield Hancock's Grant's II Corps, comprised of fifteen thousand men attacked the Mule Shoe salient. Hancock's men stormed over the Rebel earthworks.

At 5:30 p.m., Confederate General John B. Gordon's three brigades charged the Union line in an effort to retake the line. Two of Confederate General Robert Rode's brigades on Gordon's left also attacked Hancock's men and pushed them back into the Mule Shoe. The Union troops could go no further, and both sides settled into the mazes of trenches and fired into each other.[cxxvi]

During the battle, Cowan moved his battery to the Landrum house, which was located near the Mule Shoe salient. Cowan marched his guns for about a mile, and while moving his guns was exposed to enemy fire, but received no damage. Cowan placed four guns at the Landrum house. The rest of Cowan's guns, under Lieutenant Van Etten, parked behind the Landrum house with the caissons. The Confederates under Gordon attacked the Union lines, and the fire concentrated at an angle six hundred yards from the Landrum's house. A Union battery left their position two hundred yards from Cowan's position, so Cowan placed a section of his battery, under Van Etten, to fill in the gap. Colonel Thompkins sent a section of three brass guns to assist Cowan. After dark, Cowan entrenched, but the Confederates retired for the night.[cxxvii]

During the battle, Union General Horatio Wright's IV Corps attacked the Rebel works reoccupied by General Robert Rode's men on the left of the salient. The Union soldiers managed to occupy breastworks at a section of the line that formed a sharp angle, but could not advance any further. Both sides were only yards apart when they poured volley after volley into each other. Rain began to fall and quickly filled the trenches with water. For twenty hours, the battle raged on and many of the wounded men who piled up in the trenches drowned in the trenches. In one twelve by fifteen foot section of the angle, over 150 men were dead. So many bullets hit the dead bodies that they simply fell apart into masses. The area became known as "The Bloody Angle." Union losses in the Battle of Spotsylvania amounted to 10,920 men killed, wounded, or missing. Confederate losses amounted to six thousand men killed, wounded or missing and nearly four thousand captured.[cxxviii]

On May 13, Cowan went on a reconnaissance with General James Rickett's division, but did not advance beyond the Union skirmish line. The rebel infantry were found nearby. Cowan marched with the brigade at night to Willis's Creek, on the Fredericksburg and Spotsylvania Roads. He moved further to Anderson's farm. The battery camped with the First Division. The Confederate infantry tried to attack the wagon train, but were repulsed. During the different engagements, Cowan fired 708 rounds. During the Battle of Spotsylvania, Cowan lost three men.[cxxix]

On May 18, General Grant moved around Lee's right flank and attacked the Confederate lines. Grant sent six of his divisions forward in a frontal attack through the Mule Shoe salient, charging over open ground towards a new Confederate line stretched across the base of the salient. Twenty-nine Confederate cannons opened up on the oncoming Union lines. Accurate Confederate rifle fire poured into the Union lines, which sent the Federal soldiers retreating. By 10:00 a.m., the attack was over, with two thousand Union soldiers lost during the battle.[cxxx]

On May 19, General Lee ordered Confederate General Richard Ewell's II Corps to advance on the Union right flank and attack Grant's wagon trains and communications in the Union rear. Ewell's six thousand men crossed the Ni River and advanced into the Union right rear. Although Ewell did not know the situation, Grant's forces had been reinforced with 7,500 Union soldiers, six thousand of the Union soldiers were from the Heavy Artillery regiments that were defending Washington, D.C. Ewell ran into a division of heavy artillery. The Battle of Harris Farm erupted upon the landscape. Union reinforcements forced Ewell to retreat. Ewell lost nine hundred men during the attack. Union losses amounted to 1,535. Grant's movement was delayed by a day.[cxxxi]

On May 20, Lee ordered his troops to pull out of Spotsylvania lines. The next day, on May 21, Grant pulled his troops out of the entrenchments. Grant hoped to pull Lee away from the entrenchments and wage a battle out in the open. Grant felt that his opportunity would come at the North Anna River, just north of where two Confederate railways crossed at Hanover Junction. Lee felt that his best opportunity to attack Grant would come as the Army of the Potomac crossed the North Anna River. At 10:00 p.m., Cowan's battery left their position on Willis' Creek, and with the brigade marched to the south side of North Anna Road.[cxxxii]

On May 22, Lee arrived at North Anna River. Lee placed his men on the south bank of the river, covering three crossings: the ford at Jericho Mills on the left, Ox Ford in the center, and Chesterfield

Cowan as a college student. Courtesy of the National Archives.

Andrew Cowan in uniform. Courtesy of the the Louisville Courier-Journal.

Siege of Yorktown, Virginia. Courtesy of the Library of Congress.

Siege of Yorktown. Courtesy of the Library of Congress.

Battle of Williamsburg. Courtesy of the Library of Congress.

Battle of Williamsburg. Courtesy of the Library of Congress.

The bridge at Antietam, Maryland. Courtesy of the Library of Congress.

View of Dunker Church after the Battle of Antietam. Courtesy of the Library of Congress.

Burnside Brigde, Antietam, Maryland. Courtesy of the Library of Congress.

Burnside Bridge. Courtesy of the Library of Congress.

Burnside Bridge. Courtesy of the Library of Congress.

Dunker Church, Antietam. Courtesy of the Library of Congress.

Sunken Lane or Bloody Lane, Antietam. Courtesy of the Library of Congress.

Sunken Lane or Bloody Lane, Antietam. Courtesy of the Library of Congress.

Sunken Lane or Bloody Lane, Antietam. Courtesy of the Library of Congress.

Battle of Five Forks. Courtesy of the Library of Congress.

Battle of Fredericksburg. Courtesy of the Library of Congress.

Battle of Fredericksburg. Courtesy of the Library of Congress.

Fredericksburg. Courtesy of the Library of Congress.

Chancellorsville. Courtesy of the Library of Congress.

Caisson and limber chests, Gettysburg, Pennsylvania. Located near the Bloody Angle. Photo courtesy of the author.

The Bloody Angle at Gettysburg. Photo courtesy of the author.

The memorial at the copse of trees at Gettysburg. Cowan's battery was to the left of the trees. Photo courtesy of the author.

The Eternal Light Peace Memorial at Gettysburg. Photo courtesy of the author.

View of the field from the Union side and Pickett and Pettigrew's men marched across the open field from Seminary Ridge. Photo courtesy of the author.

The corpse of trees, Cowan's monument is to the left. Courtesy of the Library of Congress.

Petersburg, Virginia. Captain Andrew Cowan's 1st New York Independent Battery Light Artillery within Confederate works on the Petersburg line, April 1865. Courtesy of the Library of Congress.

Cowan's independent battery, 1st N.Y., inside one of the rebel forts in front of Petersburg, 24th June 1864. Courtesy of the Library of Congress.

Interior view of Rebel fort in front of Petersburg works, manned by Cowan's Independent battery, 1st N.Y., 24th June, 1864. Courtesy of the Library of Congress.

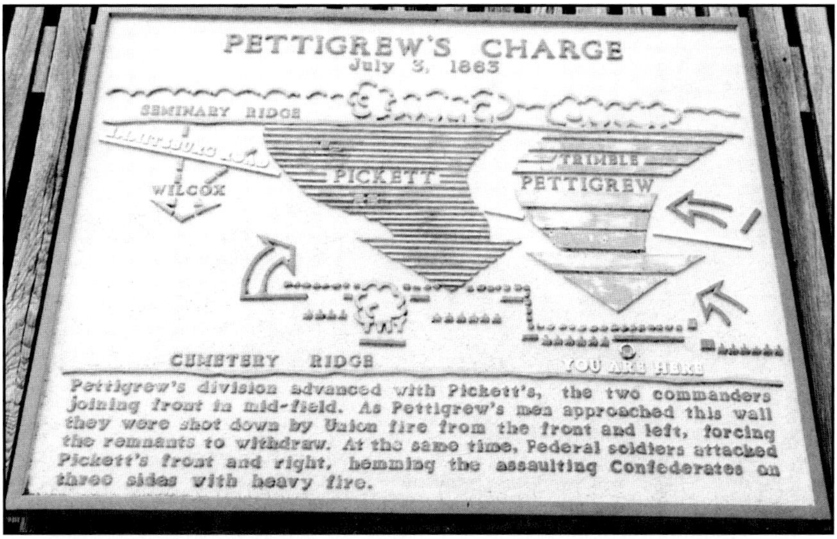

Cowan's battery is to the left of the trees on Cemetery Ridge. Photo courtesy of the author.

Andrew Cowan's grave, Cave Hill Cemetery. Photo courtesy of the author.

Battle of Cold Harbor. Courtesy of the Library of Congress.

Cold Harbor. Courtesy of the Library of Congress

Battle of Spotsylvania. Courtesy of the Library of Congress.

Battle of Spotsylvania. Courtesy of the Library of Congress.

Battle of Spotsylvania. Courtesy of the Library of Congress.

North Anna Campaign. Courtesy of the Library of Congress.

Fort Stevens, Washington, D.C. Courtesy of the Library of Congress.

Fort Stevens, dedication marker to where Lincoln was observing the fighting on July 11, 1864. Courtesy of the Library of Congress.

Fort Stevens, Washington, D.C. Courtesy of the Library of Congress.

Charge of Hancock, Spotsylvania. Courtesy of the Library of Congress.

McClean House, Appomattox. Courtesy of the Library of Congress.

General Royemn Ayres. Courtesy of the Library of Congress.

Three inch Ordnance Rifle, similar to what Cowan used during the Civil War. Courtesy of the The Civil War Battles of the Western Theater Museum, Bardstown, Kentucky.

Col. Charles H. Tompkins. MOLLUS

General Henry Hunt, Chief of Artillery during the Battle of Fredericksburg. Courtesy of the Library of Congress.

Union General Alexander Webb. Courtesy of the Library of Congress.

First on the left is Andrew Cowan (later brevet-lieutenant-colonel), then lieutenant commanding the battery (he had been promoted to captain at Lee's Mills, but had not yet received his captain's commission). Next is First-Lieutenant William P. Wright (who was disabled for life by wounds received in the battle of Gettysburg), Lieutenant William H. Johnson (wounded at Gettysburg and mortally wounded at Winchester), and Lieutenant Theodore Atkins, sun struck during the fierce cannonade at Gettysburg, July 3, 1863, and incapacitated for further service in the army. Private Henry Hiser, in charge of the officers' mess at the time, is leaning against the tent pole. Photograph in Frank Miller's Photographic History of the Civil War, 1912.

Union General Winfield Hancock. Courtesy of the Library of Congress.

Gen. William Smith. Courtesy of the Library of Congress.

Example of a Bormann time fuze. Photograph Courtesy of The Civil War Battles of the Western Theater Museum, Bardstown, Kentucky. Photograph Courtesy of the Civil War Battles of the Western Theater Museum, Bardstown, Kentucky.

12-pounder Smoothbore Canister shell. Photograph Courtesy of the Civil War Battles of the Western Theater Museum, Bardstown, Kentucky.

10-pounder Parrott Rifle projectile. Photograph Courtesy of the Civil War Battles of the Western Theater Museum, Bardstown, Kentucky.

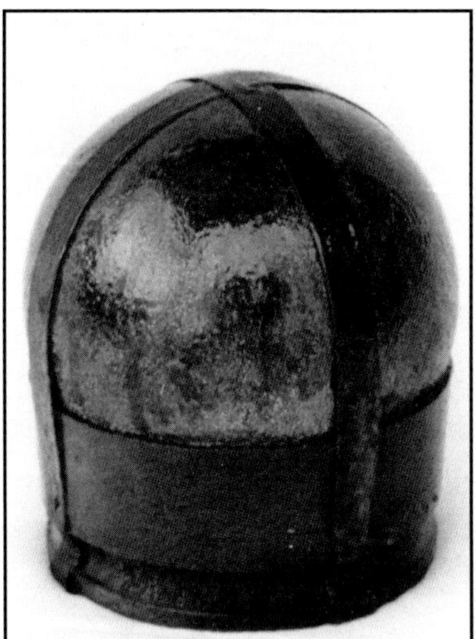

12-pounder Solid Shot projectile. Photograph courtesy of the Civil War Battles of the Western Theater, Bardstown, Kentucky.

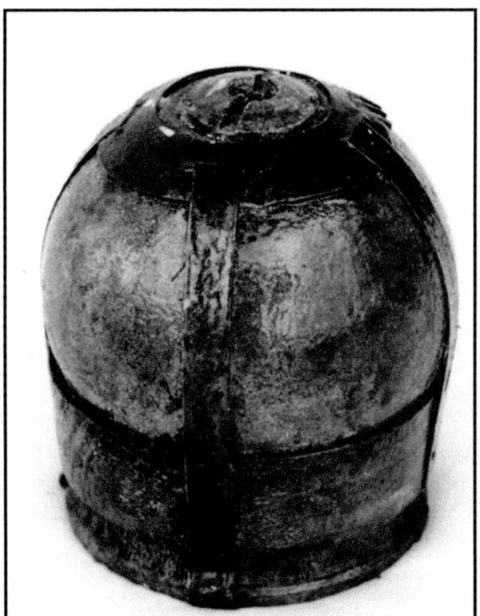

12-pounder Spherical Case (Shrapnel Shell) projectile. Photograph courtesy of the Civil War Battles of the Western Theater, Bardstown, Kentucky.

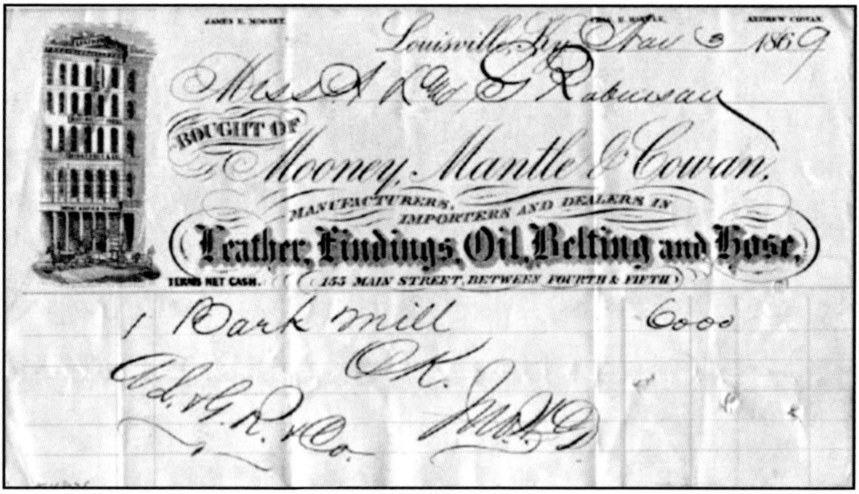
Louisville, Ky. 1869

BOUGHT OF

Mooney, Mantle & Cowan,

MANUFACTURERS, IMPORTERS AND DEALERS IN

Leather, Findings, Oil, Belting and Hose,

TERMS NET CASH. 155 MAIN STREET, BETWEEN FOURTH & FIFTH

1 Bark mill 6000

Mooney, Mantle & Cowan invoice from 1869. Courtesy of the Kentucky Historical Society.

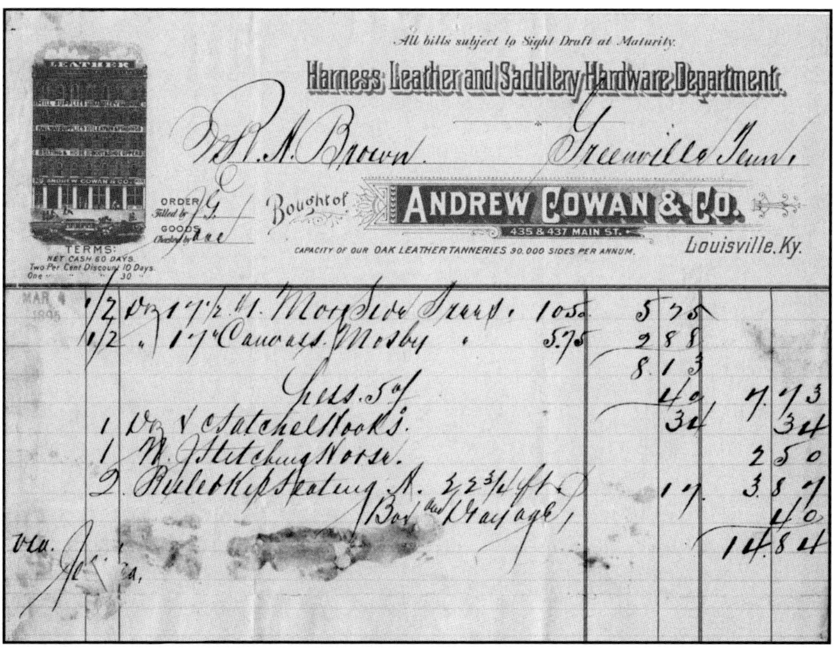
All bills subject to Sight Draft at Maturity.

Harness Leather and Saddlery Hardware Department.

Bought of ANDREW COWAN & CO.

435 & 437 MAIN ST.

CAPACITY OF OUR OAK LEATHER TANNERIES 30,000 SIDES PER ANNUM.

Louisville, Ky.

ORDER Filled by

GOODS Checked by

TERMS:
NET CASH 60 DAYS.
Two Per Cent Discount 10 Days.
One " " 30 "

Andrew Cowan & Co. invoice from March 1895. Courtesy of the author's personal collection.

1895 29th Encampment Souvenir. Courtesy of the Author's personal collection.

Grand Army of the Republic 1895 ribbon. Courtesy of the Author's personal collection.

Battle of Chickamauga 1895 dedication ribbon. Courtesy of the Author's personal collection.

"Old Kentucky" National Encampment G.A.R. in favor of Louisville, 1895 ribbon. Courtesy of the Author's personal collection.

1895 Silver plated souvenir spoon from the 1895 G.A.R. reunion. Courtesy of the Author's personal collection.

1895 G.A.R. canteen with G.A.R. hat cord. "We Drank from the Same Canteen." Courtesy of the Author's personal collection.

Lincoln Memorial Hodgenville Kentucky. Courtesy of the National Park Service.

Andrew Cowan. Courtesy of the Library of Congress.

Iroquois Park Overlook in 1919. Courtesy of the University of Louisville Digital Archives.

Iroquois Park in 1921 of the Observation Point. Courtesy of the University of Louisville Digital Archives.

Cherokee Bridge, located in Cherokee Park. Photo courtesy of the author.

Hogan Fountain, located in Cherokee Park. Photo courtesy of the author.

Alloway House, Cowan's French Tudor style house. Photo courtesy of the author.

Bridge on the right. On May 23, Union General Gouverneur Warren arrived and pushed his men across the river just west of Jericho Mills and advanced for a half mile when he was attacked by Confederate General C. M. Wilcox's division. The battle came to an end when heavy rains poured onto the battlefield. Union General Winfield Hancock assaulted the Confederates and managed to take the crossing at Chesterfield Bridge.[cxxxiii]

On May 24, Cowan was ordered to build earthworks, and placed his guns in position near the house of Edwin Anderson, on the Little River. On that same day, Grant's army crossed over the river on each flank. Lee ordered his men to entrench and erected earthworks. Lee hoped to concentrate his forces to attack one of the Union flanks, but he came down with an intestinal disorder and was not able to launch an offensive. Lee's opportunity to attack Grant's flank slipped by and Grant was able to strengthen his position.[cxxxiv]

On May 25, Cowan withdrew his guns from Little River and recrossed the river, marching his guns to Chesterfield Station. On May 26, Grant pulled his men back across the river. The next day, on May 27, Cowan's guns left Chesterfield Station and marched with the brigade across the Pamunkey River.

By May 30, Cowan was entrenched at Totopotomoy Creek. On June 1, Confederate General Joseph Kershaw's two infantry brigades charged across open fields to attack the Union position at Cold Harbor. Union General Phil Sheridan's dismounted cavalry fired into the oncoming Confederates. The 20th South Carolina regiment under the command of Colonel Lawrence Keitt fled after Sheridan's men fired Spencer carbines into his command. More Rebel regiments attacked the Union regiments, but again the Spencer carbines put the Rebel charges to a halt. By midday, Confederate General Richard Anderson's four divisions planned another attack. The Union reinforcements arrived under the command of General Horatio Wright's VI Corps. By 4:00 p.m., General William F. Smith's XVIII Corps arrived to support Wright. Cowan's battery fell in with the First Division. Cowan shelled the Confederate earthworks beyond the Totopotomoy. The Rebels replied with 20-pound Parrott rifles, but caused no damage to the Union guns.[cxxxv]

On June 2, Cowan built works for his guns on the left of Gaines Mill Road, in rear of the extreme right of the Second Corps. He placed his guns in the works constructed by his men, and came under fire from Confederate sharpshooters.[cxxxvi] On that same day, General Grant planned a massive attack on the Rebel lines at Cold Harbor. At 5:00 p.m., six Union divisions struck Anderson's four divisions and almost carried the Rebel position, but the Union attack was repulsed with the loss of 2,200 men.[cxxxvii]

At 4:00 p.m. on June 3, fifty thousand Union soldiers from three corps, including the right of the Second Corps, advanced in a two-mile long line towards the Rebel earthworks. The Confederate earthworks were covered with cannons and rifles. The Confederates held their fire until the Union soldiers were within deadly range, and then fired into the front ranks with volleys of canister and rifle fire. Cowan did not realize that the Union infantry had made a charge until he saw the infantry leaving their rifle pits. He opened fire on the rebel line, silencing their guns, which were playing havoc on the Union infantry. The first Union line went down and the second line stepped over the bodies of the first line as they advanced. The second line was swept away by the storm of bullets and canister. In a half hour, the Union troops suffered seven thousand men. The thirty thousand Confederates who were involved in the battle suffered on 1,500 men.[cxxxviii]

After the battle of Cold Harbor, Cowan remained in his position until June 12, firing at the rebels when he had the opportunity. That night, Cowan withdrew his guns, destroyed the earthworks and marched to the James River. He lost one commissioned officer, four enlisted men, and a few horses. He fired 325 rounds during the engagement.[cxxxix] The Union defeat at Cold Harbor on June 3rd put an end to any major fighting. During Grant's twenty-eight day Overland Campaign, the Army of the Potomac lost 50,000 men. Grant was not able to destroy General Lee's Army of Northern Virginia or capture the Confederate capital, but unlike other Union generals, Grant continued to fight Lee. During the Overland Campaign, Grant would never retreat.[cxl]

Chapter 9

Confederate General Jubal Early's Washington Raid

On June 13, Cowan marched with the brigade and crossed the Chickahominy River. By June 15, General James Ricketts placed his battery near the James River, crossed the James River by pontoon bridges, and marched towards Petersburg. On June 18, Cowan placed his guns in Battery Number 5, where he remained until June 21, engaging the Confederate batteries beyond the Appomattox. On June 21, he moved with the corps to the left on the Jerusalem Plank Road. He marched with the brigade to Ream's Station, and followed them to City Point where he loaded his guns aboard the steamers *Disney* and *Star*.

On June 23, 1864, General Jubal Early's fourteen thousand Confederate soldiers began their march down the Shenandoah Valley. Union General David Hunter's Union army withdrew beyond the Allegany Mountains, leaving Washington, D.C. exposed. General Jubal Early's men marched north, hoping to force General Ulysses S. Grant to detach part of his army to defend the capital. On July 2, the Confederates entered Winchester, where Early decided to divide his army, sending one force against Harpers Ferry while the second force continued toward Martinsburg, West Virginia. By July 5, the Confederate army was camped beyond the Potomac River. Early received ordered from General Lee to detach a cavalry brigade towards Baltimore to cut communications and assist in a plan to free eighteen thousand prisoners of war from Point Lookout, Maryland. On July 8, Early crossed South Mountain and entered Frederick.

Just east of Frederick, Early attacked Union General Lew Wallace's men five times before withdrawing. By July 11, Early's men reached the defenses of Washington, D.C. in front of Fort Stevens. The Third Division of the Sixth Corps, including Cowan's battery, under the command of General Rickett's, was shipped from City Point to Baltimore and marched out to reinforce Wallace at Monacy in Maryland.[cxli] Rickett's men held Early back for forty-eight hours, which gave the Second Division of the Sixth Corps time to reach Washington just as Early had arrived before the undefended forts. The steamer carrying Cowan's artillery and horses was the first to arrive after the infantry. Cowan was met with orders to march to Fort Stevens. When Cowan arrived at the Fort, the infantry already engaged the Confederates in the valley below the Union army and Cowan had orders to halt and wait developments. Cowan saw General Wright, Cowan's Corps commander, standing on a parapet of Fort Stevens, to Cowan's left, watching the fighting that was going on, and at his side Cowan recognized President Lincoln. Numerous bullets from the Confederates struck in dust on the road where the Union troops were waiting, and many fell were the President stood with General Wright, yet Lincoln did not move. Cowan learned later that General Wright had begged Lincoln not to expose himself, but he paid no attention to his advice.[cxlii]

Early planned to assault Fort Stevens on July 12, but the lead elements of the VI Corps arrived at Fort Stevens during the night and morning, changed his plans and he decided to resume his skirmishing. Lincoln visited the fort again and once more came under fire. During the exchange, a young Union officer, Captain Oliver Wendell Holmes, Jr. seeing the President watching the battle, shouted: "Get down, you fool." Lincoln meekly complied with the order.[cxliii] During the night of July 12 and July 13, the Confederates abandoned their raid, marching south toward Virginia. Early knew that a frontal assault against the well-manned defenses of Washington would prove disastrous and rode back to the safety of Confederates lines. Although he was not able to release the prisoners from Point Lookout, Maryland, he was able to accomplish his plan of relieving pressure on the Confederate forces defending Petersburg.

On July 15, Cowan was detached from the brigade at Poolesville and ordered to, along with two regiments of the First Division, to Young's Island and placed his guns in position, while the cavalry, under Colonel Lowell, crossed the river. Cowan rejoined the VI Corps at White's Ford, and was attached to the Second Division.[cxliv]

On July 27, Cowan marched with the division from the vicinity of Washington to Hyattstown, and the next day marched to Jefferson, through Monocacy. On July 29, Cowan marched to Harpers Ferry and crossed the Potomac River, camping near Halltown. The next day,

Cowan's battery re-crossed the Potomac River into Maryland. From May 4 to July 30, Cowan lost one commissioned officer, and seven enlisted men wounded. He fired a total of 1,158 rounds.[cxlv]

Chapter 10

The Shenandoah Valley Campaign

During the first week of August, Union General Ulysses S. Grant came to the conclusion that a successful end to the war in Virginia relied on victory in the Shenandoah Valley and destruction of the region. He combined four overlapping Union departments into the Middle Military District and on August 6, he replaced General Hunter with Major General Phil Sheridan. General Sheridan organized the newly formed Army of the Shenandoah, with 40,000 men. The army included the VI Corps, to which Cowan's battery was attached, two divisions of the XIX Corps, the Army of West Virginia, and three cavalry divisions, two of which were moved from Petersburg to the new Army of the Shenandoah. Sheridan would be engaging Confederate General Jubal Early's Army of the Valley, which numbered 12,000 men, and comprised of four infantry divisions, two artillery battalions, and two cavalry divisions.[cxlvi]

Sheridan advanced his army up the valley. Early withdrew to a strong defensive position at Fisher's Hill. The two forces skirmished until Sheridan ordered a withdrawal. Lee sent an additional infantry and a cavalry division with additional artillery battalion to assist Early. Early arrived opposite Sheridan's left flank, and he decided to withdraw north. During the next two months, both sides skirmished along the Opequon Creek, which flowed into the Potomac River. On September 13, 1864, Cowan was severely injured in a skirmish near Gilbert's Ford on Opequon Creek. He received a brevet for his action during the battle. After his injury, Cowan's battery was turned over to Lieutenant W.H. Johnson.[cxlvii]

When Atlanta, Georgia fell to Union forces on September 2, 1864, President Lincoln gave Grant permission to allow Sheridan to advance his army, which he did on September 19. Cowan and the First New York Independent Battery marched towards Winchester and halted in a ravine for an hour, and then ordered into position about a mile from the Confederate forces. The Union infantry formed into line of battle, with the Second Division on the left, with the Third Division next in line, and then the First Division in reserve, with the First New York Independent Battery, under Lieutenant W.H. Johnson, on the right. The remaining artillery was brought up and three other batteries, namely the Fifth Maine, Battery M, Fifth U.S. Artillery, and C, First Rhode Island Light Artillery, placed in position on the Corp's front by the chief of artillery, Colonel C.H. Tompkins. The 19th Corps, under General Emory, was on the right of the pike, connecting with the Sixth Corps.

Confederate batteries shelled the First New York Independent battery for an hour, but Johnson's men also shelled the Confederate's batteries. At 9:00 a.m., the Union infantry advanced and the First New York Independent battery advanced with them for about 1,200 yards and came into position within close range of the Confederates. While getting into position, Lieutenant Johnson was shot through the leg and Lieutenant Orsamus Van Etten took command of the battery. At 11:40 a.m., the Sixth and Nineteenth Corps advanced, driving the Confederates before them. Early's Confederates charged the left of the 19th Corps, driving them back, and then turned on the flank of the 3rd Division, Sixth Corps, and threatened a disaster. Wright sent in the reserve of the 6th Corps, and directed Colonel Tompkins to hold two of his batteries in position and turn on the advancing Confederates. Van Etten held the battery in position as long as the infantry held their line in front of his front, and then they fell back. Van Etten fell back with them, drawing the pieces by hand until the rise of the ground gave him some protection, then he limbered up his pieces. He moved to the rear two hundred yards away and took position on the rise of ground just in the rear of the infantry line.

Once unlimbered, Etten preceded to fire on the advancing Confederates. One of the guns broke an axel from the recoil of the gun, and was sent to the rear. General Crook advanced on the Confederate's left, and Wright ordered forward the 19th and Sixth Corps. The Confederates were driven off at all points toward and beyond Winchester.[cxlviii] After the infantry's charge was successful, Cowan's battery was able to rest for an hour. Soon Van Etten was ordered to be ready for follow up another attack. As the troops advanced, Cowan's battery moved forward to the same position they had fallen back from. Van Etten did not open fire, for fear of hitting the advancing Union army. General Wright of the VI Corps ordered Etten to move his battery to the pike toward Winchester, about 1,200 yards away. While getting into position, the battery came under heavy fire. Van Etten fired back, and was ordered to continue firing until the Confederates seized firing, then he moved his battery toward Winchester. He halted one mile from town and about dark, was ordered to park for the night, about a half mile from town. The Union infantry reached Winchester, and the Confederates made a stand on the Strasburg Road, and the 19th and 6th Corps changed front with the intent of attacking again, but the Confederates fell back and darkness ended the battle. During the battle, the artillery batteries fired eighteen wagon loads of ammunition. Sheridan lost more than five thousand men.[cxlix] Confederate General Early lost 3,500 men. The battle of Opequon Creek would also be known as the Third Battle of Winchester. During the battle, Van Etten lost six men, wounded, two horses killed, and two wounded. He also fired 585 rounds of fixed ammunition, 195 percussion, 260 case shot, and 120 timed fuses.[cl]

On September 20, the First New York Independent battery moved towards Strasburg, fifteen miles, and camped. Two days later, on September 22, Union General George Crook moved his corps beyond the Confederate left and charged. The rest of the Federal infantry charged the front of the earthworks at Fisher's Hill and the Confederates broke under the Union attack. The First New York Independent battery went into position and fired five shots, and moved closed to the Confederate forces and opened fire. After holding his position for a short time, he moved out and took position on the right of the Sixth Corps batteries. From this point, Van Etten fired his guns by sections. Night ended the battle. He fired 105 rounds during the engagement, and did not lose any men or horses. The battle of Fisher's Hill was a success for Sheridan's Army of West Virginia.[cli]

At 4:00 a.m., Van Etten halted for one hour, then moved through Woodstock and again halted, ate breakfast and drew rations. On September 24, he received orders to move out. He moved through Mount Jackson and halted at 1:00 p.m., where he was ordered to follow the skirmish line that was advancing. He pushed on as fast as possible until New Market, when he turned to the right to take position 250 yards from the pike, firing a few rounds at the retreating Confederates. Wright then ordered him to report to Captain Taft, of the 19th Corps, with one section, and Van Etten followed the Rebels from one rise of the ground to another, coming into position four times, and firing a few shots each time. The other section of the battery moved along the pike until the last position, then joined the section engaged and came in position with it. Darkness brought an end to the fighting, after following the Confederates for eight miles. He rejoined the VI Corps and camped for the night, having fired 180 rounds.[clii]

On September 25, Van Etten received orders to move out at once and rode to Harrisonburg and camped. On September 28, the First Independent battery received orders to move out and rode to Mount Crawford. On September 30, the battery moved back to their old camp in Harrisonburg. On October 6, he moved beyond New Market and the next day the battery moved to Woodstock. On October 8, the battery moved to Strasburg. On October 10, Van Etten received orders to report to General Wheaton of the 1st Division and moved through Middletown and camped near Front Royal for the night. On October 11, Van Etten received orders to report to General Bidwell, cross the river, and camped near the town. On October 13, Van Etten rejoined the corps, moved towards Winchester, then Millwood, when he was ordered to turn around and camp near Millwood. On October 14, Etten received orders to move to Newtown, then Middletown.[cliii]

On October 19, Confederate General Early led a surprise attack on the Union army. Van Etten was awakened by musketry and ordered to harness his horses. He ordered his guns into position about two hundred yards from his camp, then Tompkins ordered him to a rise of ground, as the infantry were falling back. The Confederates routed the Union forces and pushed them back beyond Middletown. Union General Sheridan arrived to the front and managed to rally his men and at 4:00 p.m., he led a counterattack and routed the Confederates.

During the battle, Van Etten was in the process of limbering his cannons when the infantry rallied, so he unlimbered and began to fire as rapidly as possible. He held his position until the infantry fell back, then he fell back with them, having one cannon disabled with a broken axle. He lost one officer and six men killed, and sixteen wounded and ten horses killed. He moved to the rear about a mile, and managed to get one section in fighting order, and sent the section back to the front. Before he reached the position, he was ordered back to get the battery together. Van Etten was ordered to move his pieces near the pike. He readied his pieces for action and moved along the pike to within one mile of Middletown, and waited for orders. When orders came two hours later, he moved his battery forward and to the right, and went into position 1,400 yards from Middletown. He fired until the Union infantry advanced, then he was ordered forward, and moved to the top of the crest from Cedar Creek, and then ordered back to the camp they had left in the morning. He fired 55 timed shells, 45 case shot, 39 percussion shell, and 15 combination. He lost one officer and five men killed, and seventeen wounded, twelve horses killed and six disabled.[cliv] The battle of Cedar Creek was Sheridan's last major battle during the Shenandoah Campaign. Through the fall and winter, both Sheridan and Early returned most of their armies to their commanders at Petersburg. The Shenandoah Valley Campaign marked the beginning of the end for the Confederacy in Virginia. The Union army's destruction of the valley ensured that the Confederates could no longer rely on the fall harvests for food to feed their ever dwindling army. The campaign was one of the most decisive of the war.[clv]

Chapter 11

The Appomattox Campaign

The Appomattox campaign was the last major campaign in which Cowan's guns were involved. After recovering from his wounds from the Gilbert's Creek in September of 1864, he took command of the VI Corps artillery outside of Petersburg. The Union army command placed Cowan in charge of an artillery brigade and brevetted him a lieutenant colonel. During the month of March 1865, Cowan managed to break away from the entrenchments at Petersburg and attend a reception in the White House in Washington, D.C. The highlight of the reception was when Cowan shook hands with President Abraham Lincoln. A month later, the President would be assassinated.[clvi]

After the battle of Cold Harbor, both the Union army and Confederate army dug entrenchments at Petersburg, and the next several months, the Union army committed themselves to a period of siege warfare. On March 23, Union General William Sherman and Union General John Schofield combined forces at Goldsboro, North Carolina. Union General Ulysses S. Grant devised a plan for another flanking attack against the Confederate right below Petersburg. By March 26, 1865, General Robert E. Lee informed President Jefferson Davis that Richmond and Petersburg were in danger of being taken by Union forces. Lee felt that he had to leave the trenches and join Confederate General Joseph Johnston and fight in another location.[clvii]

Grant expected Lee to leave the trenches and join Johnston, so he planned a movement to prevent Lee's plans. Grant ordered Union General Ord to pull out the XXIV Corps, led by General John Gibbon and General Ronald Mackenzie's cavalry division out of the Union lines north of the James River and move towards the Federal left, southwest of Petersburg. Ord's men were to relieve the II Corps and V Corps from trench duty. Once relieved by Ord, General Warren's V Corps and General Humphrey's II Corps were to march west along the Vaughan road until they marched past the Confederate flank. The Union troops would march north toward the Confederate line. The Union troops were to flank the Confederates, not to bring on an engagement. The goal was to force the Confederates out of the entrenchments, so they could protect their rear and the Southside railroad. Union General Phil Sheridan's 5,700 cavalry were to swing around the Confederate infantry to the Dinwiddie Court House, then turn north toward Five Forks.[clviii]

On March 29, General Lee pulled General George Pickett's division south of the James to help support against Union General Richard Anderson's division on the Confederate right. Lee ordered General Fitzhugh Lee's cavalry to take charge of the divisions led by General William H. F. Lee and General Thomas Rosser. The combined Confederate forces would attack Sheridan's cavalry. Lee sent General Bushrod Johnson's division to determine the strength of Warren's lead division, under the command of General Charles Griffin. Union General Joshua Lawrence Chamberlain's lead brigade encountered Confederate General Johnson's troops. Warren and Humphrey approached the Confederate trenches. Sheridan sent Merritt, with Devin's cavalry division north toward Dinwiddie to take the Five Forks. Sheridan's men ran into Fitzhugh Lee's cavalry, who arrived at Five Forks. Merritt pushed back the Confederate cavalry to Five Forks, but Sheridan's men soon discovered Pickett's division. At 2:00 p.m., Lee and Pickett drove Union General Crook's brigade and two of Devin's brigades back across the Dinwiddie Road. Pickett advanced his men south towards Dinwiddie, while Rosser's and William Lee's cavalry divisions attacked the Federals from the west. Two of Sheridan's brigades, led by Alfred Gibbs and J. Irvin Gregg, fought to hold their position on the Dinwiddie Road, but the Confederates drove them south. Sheridan ordered two new brigades to join his force and formed a defensive line, fighting broke out, but darkness put an end to the fighting.[clix]

On March 31, General Warren sent out a division under General Romeyn Ayres to find out how well the Confederate defended the White Oaks Road. Warren's men walked into Anderson's flanking attack. Ayre's brigades collapsed under the Confederate fire. Warren's division, under the command of General Griffin, heard the fighting and moved toward the action. Griffin halted the Confederate advance. On the Union right, General Nelson Miles led his division of the II Corps joined the fight and regained lost ground. By mid-afternoon, Warren ordered a counterattack, led by Chamberlain's brigade. Chamberlain led his brigade into a charge that advanced towards the White Oak Road. Warren sent a brigade to help the fighting on the Dinwiddie Court House. At 8:40 p.m., Warren decided to move his entire corps west and attack the Confederates on one side while Sheridan attacked the other side. Warren would send Griffin's men down the Boydton Plank Road to support Sheridan and take his other two divisions around the Confederate rear.[clx]

By daylight the next day, Pickett retreated, followed by Union General Merritt's cavalry. Pickett fell back to his entrenchments at the White Oak Road, centered on Five Forks. Sheridan devised a plan where his cavalry would fight dismounted and keep Pickett's men occupied while Warren's infantry would attack the Confederate left. Pickett anticipated the flanking movement and moved his men at a forty-five degree angle to the main Union line. General Crawford's division would attack the Confederate breastworks, while General Ayres' division would attack the left. Griffin's division would support Crawford's attack. At 4:15 p.m., the V Corps attacked, with Ayre's division attacking the Confederates on the left. Crawford's men marched west through some woods, far behind the Confederate line. Ayres pushed forward. General Warren looked for Crawford's men. Warren attacked from the south. With the Rebel troops being attacked from three different sides, the line fell apart, and Ayres' and Griffin's men climbed over the angle. The Confederate left fell apart, and were being driven west. Crawford cut off Pickett's escape route. Merritt's cavalry attacked Pickett from the south and pushed the Confederates back. Pickett made a final stand and his rear guard fired on Crawford's men. Warren led a charge and Crawford's men pushed back the Confederates. By 6:45 p.m., the Confederate line collapsed. Merritt's men advanced from the south, General George Custer's two brigades charged from the west, and Mackenzie's cavalry attacked from the east, routing Fitzhugh Lee's cavalry. The Union forces captured five thousand Confederates. By 7:00 p.m., darkness ended the battle.[clxi]

With the success of Five Forks, Grant decided to attack the Petersburg entrenchments. Meade ordered Generals Wright and Parke to attack the entrenchments on April 2. Brevet Major Cowan, who was commanding the artillery brigade, received orders from the Sixth

Corps that they would assault the rebel works at 4:00 a.m. the next morning, and five batteries of the brigade would assist in the major assault. Cowan commanded Battery E, Fifth U.S. Artillery, 3rd New York Independent Battery, Battery H, First Rhode Island Artillery, First New York Independent Battery, with Captain O.R. Van Etten commanding Cowan's battery, and Battery G, First Rhode Island Battery. At 10:00 p.m., General Wright ordered the batteries to open fire on the rebel lines, and the Union batteries fired for about three hours.[clxii]

At 2:00 a.m. in the morning, on April 2, the batteries selected to accompany the Union assault were relieved from their position in the works and massed near Fort Fisher.

Brevet Major G. W. Adams, along with twenty men, advanced with the assaulting column to take command of and turn the Confederate guns should the assault prove successful. A section of Captain Allen's battery, under Lieutenant Walter M. Knight, advanced with General Frank Wheaton's division in front of Fort Welch, and opened fire on the rebels. When news came that the Union assault proved successful, Major Adams and his detachment succeeded in turning some of the rebel guns on the retreating Confederates. Two enlisted men were injured during the assault.[clxiii]

The Third New York Battery, under Major William Ham and a section of Battery G, First Rhode Island Artillery, were placed in position with the advance of the Third Division and opened a heavy fire on a point that the Confederates still held, succeeding in silencing one of their batteries. The Third New York battery advanced with the Second and Third Division to where the Twenty-fourth Corps formed a junction with the Sixth Corps and helped drive the enemy off the field. The rebel works in that direction were either carried by the Union infantry or abandoned. The Union line advanced towards Petersburg, the Third New York Battery accompanying the Second Division, taking several positions as the rebels retreated and helped drive the Confederates from their positions. Casualties included two enlisted men wounded, and one horse killed. Battery H, First Rhode Island Artillery, advanced with the troops, and helped drive back the Confederates, but the battery became entangled in a cross fire from rebel rifled guns. Three men were killed and six wounded, and ten horses killed.[clxiv]

After Union troops took the rebel works, the reserve batteries were sent in front of the Union works. General John Gibbon ordered a section of the First New York Battery to be placed in position under the fire of a Confederate battery. After firing seventy rounds, the battery succeeded in silencing the guns. The whole battery moved toward Petersburg and took position near the Whitworth house, opening fire on the Confederate infantry. The battery came under severe fire from rebel sharpshooters. The battery opened on one of the rebel forts, and the rebels fired back but with no damage. The fire continued until dark, and the battery fired 611 rounds. Two men were wounded and two horses disabled.[clxv]

Battery E, Fifth US Artillery moved with the Third Division and took position in front of the rebel works known as Fort McGraw and Battery 45, and fired rapidly.

On April 2, all the batteries were entrenched and took position with orders to fire on the Confederates at five o'clock the following morning, but the rebels had already fled.

During the battle, fourteen thousand Union soldiers from the VI Corps prepared for battle southwest of Petersburg. Parke's IX Corps reached the entrenchments first, attacking Confederate General John B. Gordon's corps at Fort Mahone. By 9:00 a.m., General Robert Potter's division captured Fort Mahone and the surrounding trenches, but the Confederates rallied and pushed back the Union troops. On the Confederate right, Wright's VI Corps breached the entrenchments and the Confederates were driven from their entrenchments. Wright's men continued over the Boyton Plank Road to the Southside Railroad a mile away. Wright's men turned towards Hatcher's Run. Wright joined General John Gibbon's XXIV Corps and Gibbon headed towards Petersburg.[clxvi] Confederate General Robert E. Lee knew that Petersburg was lost. He sent a telegram to Secretary of War, John C. Breckinridge, to leave Richmond. President Davis would have to leave the capital of the Confederacy. The remainder of the Confederate forces retreated to Appomattox. Richmond was soon abandoned.[clxvii]

Lee's Army of Northern Virginia arrived at Amelia Court House. By April 4, Crook's cavalry and Griffin's V Corps had reached Jetersville, directly in front of Lee's army. Humphry's II Corps and Wright's VI Corps approached Jetersville. On April 5, Lee left Amelia Court House and marched towards Rice's Station. By April 6, Confederate General Longstreet was five miles from Rice's Station.[clxviii]

On April 6, Merritt's Union cavalry halted the advance of Confederate General Anderson's Corps on the Rice's Station. Confederate General Ewell formed behind Little Sayler's Creek to face Wright's VI Corps. All the Union batteries under Cowan's command took position and fired until the rebels were routed. So many of the rebel soldiers were killed or wounded from artillery fire that Cowan wrote, that such carnage had "so seldom been seen in this war in so small a space."[clxix] During the battle, the VI Corps division led by General Truman Seymour and General Frank Wheaton attacked across the creek. The brigades under Colonel Joseph Hamblin and General Warren Keifer surrounded the Confederate battle line, routing Ewell's men. Merritt's cavalry broke Anderson's line. General Richard Ewell, five other Confederate generals, and his two thousand men surrendered. Over eight thousand Confederate soldiers were captured during the battle. Lee's remaining army continued onto Appomattox Court House. Cowan's artillery brigade continued to follow the rest of VI Corps to the Appomattox Courthouse.

On April 9, at 10:30 a.m., Confederate General Robert E. Lee rode east to meet General Ulysses S. Grant to discuss surrender. Grant and Lee met at the McClean house, near Appomattox Court House. At 3:00 p.m., the two generals signed the terms of surrender and acceptance. They rose and shook hands. Lee rode back to his army. After the Union troops found out that the Army of Northern Virginia had surrendered, Union soldiers began to shout, and men began to throw their caps, coats, and blankets into the air. Cowan's battery fired four salutes of 36 guns each in honor of the surrender of Confederate General Robert E. Lee. The war was over.[clxx] When General Grant heard Cowan's artillery battery firing, he sent word to have it stopped. Grant wrote: "The Confederates were now our prisoners and we did not want to exult in their downfall….The war is over. The Rebels are our countrymen again."[clxxi] For his gallant and meritorious service during the Appomattox campaign, Cowan was brevetted a Lieutenant Colonel. After the surrender, Cowan landed at Burkesville Junction and expected to continue his march to Petersburg. As guests at his headquarters were as many surrendered Confederate officers as Cowan had room for. They came to him as his guests the morning after the surrender, and they remained with him when the news of President Lincoln's assassination came over the telegraph wires. The starting and shocking news of President Lincoln's assassination arrived and the Confederate officer's sorrow was as great as the Union army's. Cowan believed that Lincoln's death was at the zenith of his career.[clxxii]

On April 26, General Joseph Johnston surrendered to General Sherman. On May 11, President Jefferson Davis was captured in Georgia and June 2, General Kirby Smith surrendered his army.

On June 8, the entire Union army was to parade down Pennsylvania Avenue in Washington, D.C., on a Grand Review. The Army of the Potomac, VI Corps, along with Cowan's artillery brigade, was to march in the Grand Review. The troops moved from their camps at 4:00 a.m., and crossed the Long Bridge and proceeded up Maryland Avenue, and would be massed with the head of the column on Pennsylvania Avenue, at the foot of the Capitol grounds. At 9:00 a.m., the column was put in motion, along Pennsylvania Avenue, taking wheeling distance by head of the column, and passing the reviewing stand in front of the White house. When Cowan's battery approached the review stand, he dismounted and sat with President Andrew Johnson and Major General Wright, watching his battery pass by. After the review, his battery returned to their camps by way of the Aqueduct Bridge.[clxxiii]

On June 18, 1865, General Henry Hunt, chief of artillery, Army of the Potomac, wrote to Colonel Cowan:

> "In the labor and sacrifices which a successful peace required you have borne your full share, and I wish to assure you that in all your positions from the command of a battery to a brigade of artillery, I have had every reason to be satisfied with you. After the many battles and campaigns in which you have borne a conspicuous and valuable part, as attested by the Official Report, you had every right to expect promotion. The unfortunate policy which deprived the artillery of the field and staff necessary to its highest efficiency has alone prevented you from receiving the reward justly due you. Had the same service been rendered in any other arm you would have received your General's commission."[clxxiv]

Colonel Charles H. Thompkins, commanding the Artillery Brigade of the Sixth Corps, wrote to Governor Reuben E. Fenton of New York, recommending Cowan for his Colonel's promotion. He wrote:

> Captain Cowan has served under my command for the past two years, during which he has participated in all the battles of the Army of the Potomac and more recently in Sheridan's glorious campaign in the Valley, during one of the engagements of which he was severely wounded. He has ever proved himself a faithful, zealous, brave and efficient officer, displaying at times distinguished gallantry, eminently so at Gettysburg and always meriting for himself and his battery the commendation of his superior officers. I have had occasion to call the attention of the War Department to Captain Cowan's services and recommend him for promotion by brevet. I sincerely trust that an opportunity may now occur which will enable the State that he so nobly represents to confer well-earned promotion upon him."[clxxv]

General Horatio Wright, commander of the Sixth Corps, indorsed Colonel Thompkins recommendation and wrote:

> I most heartily concur in what is said within by Col. Thompkins. Captain Cowan, who has served in this corps since its organization has always shown himself to be a brave and efficient officer handling the battery admirably in action, and moreover, by his length of service as a Captain is believed to be entitled to promotion by seniority.[clxxvi]

After the Grand Review, Cowan's battery returned to Syracuse, New York and officially mustered out of service on June 23, 1865. During the war, Cowan lost two officers and twenty enlisted men killed, and five officers and thirty-five men wounded. Thirty-eight men died from disease and five were taken prisoner.

Chapter 12

The Southern Exposition and the Statue of Liberty

After the war, Cowan moved to Indianapolis, Indiana, but on July 1, 1866, he relocated to Louisville, Kentucky, and joined James E. Mooney and Charles H. Mantle in a business partnership known as Mooney, Mantle, and Cowan. The firm, located on 421 and 423 West Main Street, supplied leather, railway, and mill products. Cowan became president of the National Oak Leather Company of Louisville and vice president of the Louisville Leather Company. In September of 1867, Cowan's wife Mary died. He remarried in January 1876 to Anne, daughter of Elisha Morgan Gilbert of Utica, New York.

The Southern Exposition

In December 1881, Henry Watterson, editor of the *Louisville Courier-Journal*, put forth an idea for an exposition. In October of 1882, a committee formed to discuss the idea of an exposition with the streetcar lines, railroad officials, and proprietors of hotels. On October 18, 1882, the committee reported that the public supported the idea of an exposition. The committee recommended the formation of a stock company with a capital of $250,000 dollars. The committee would elect twenty-five men to sit on the Board of Directors. On October 25, 1882, the committee drafted the form of incorporation to raise a capital stock of $300,000 dollars, with the privilege to raise $500,000 dollars. The committee agreed to expand the board to fifty members becoming known as "The Committee of Fifty." The committee was comprised of some of Louisville's most influential men, including Andrew Cowan, S. L. Avery, Merriwether Lewis Clark, Jr., Charles Ballard, R.W. Knott, W. Snead, George H. Hall, N. Bloom, St. John Boyle, Henry Payne, H.A. Witherspoon, Andrew Buchanan, Biderman DuPont, W.R. Belnap, and Bennett Young.[clxxvii]

On October 27, the articles of incorporation named the exhibition: The Southern Exhibition at Louisville. The Committee of Fifty decided that the purpose of the Exhibition should be "to advance the material welfare of the producing classes of the South and West, to exhibit the products and resources of the Southern states to Northern and Eastern manufacturers and the implements and machines of the great industries of the former. But while the Exposition tends to embrace in its Southern exhibits all departments of Southern agriculture, forestry, mining, and commerce, special attention, prominence and consideration is given to cotton and its products, from "Seed to Loom!"[clxxviii] The Committee of Fifty appointed J.H. Lindenberger as Chairman of the Finance Committee and John E. Green as second vice president and Chairman of the Committee on Buildings and Grounds. R.W. Knott was made Chairman of the Committee on Advertising and Printing. The committee placed the opening of the exhibition on August 1, 1883 and running for one hundred days. The Committee made an offer for Mr. A. Bidermann DuPont's land near Central Park as the location of the Exposition.[clxxix]

After buying the land from Bidermann DuPont, the Committee chose the plans for the Southern Exposition building of Kenneth McDonald and Cornelius Curtain. The cost of the building was determined at $167,000 dollars. The committee approved $227,000 dollars for music, lights, and machinery for the building. By January 29, 1883, the committee managed to raise only $288,000 dollars, so they held a massive fundraiser at the opera house in Louisville, and invited the cities of New Albany and Jeffersonville, Indiana to participate. The event was a huge success and raised the money needed to complete the project.[clxxx]

On January 30, 1883, McDonald and Curtain began construction of the buildings. On March 15, 1883, lumber arrived for the carpentry work and soon the electricians and plumbers started their work on the massive structure. The contractors removed 35,000 cubic yards of ground. The first contract called for four million feet of lumber, but an additional six hundred and fifty thousand feet of lumber would be necessary for the additional buildings. Over thirty-five thousand panes of glass were used in the construction of the building and twenty-five tons of white lead. Six thousand squares of shingles were used on the roof. The main building covered ten acres and was six hundred feet wide and nine hundred feet long. Situated from the outer boundaries of the building were open courts, four in number, 945 feet by 100 feet in size. The cross shaped figure left in the center of the structure was higher than the remainder of the building, having around the outside boundary a gallery which would be used as a promenade. The central pavilion was one hundred feet square, and the corner pavilions were each ninety feet square. The curtains connecting the pavilion north and south were each 810 feet long, and those connecting east and west were 160 feet long. The central cross was four hundred feet by six hundred feet and was 110 feet wide and forty-five feet high up to the bottom of the trusses. Twenty-five feet above the first floor there were five thousand feet of galleries extending around the building.[clxxxi]

The exposition grounds covered forty-five acres, with forests and flowerbeds. The park covered eighteen acres. The Exposition ran just south of Central Park, from Fourth to Sixth Street and from Weissinger (now Park) Avenue to Hill Street. The 205 foot by 82 foot by 50 foot arched hall with a skylight access art gallery was built on the northeast section of the park, and had a fountain in the center, directly opposite from the twenty-foot wide archway entrance. The Exposition also boasted of a three thousand seat Music Hall located in the center of the park. South of the main building and east of the saw mill annex was the field agricultural exhibit, which grew every staple vegetable of the South. The field comprised about ten acres and represented a Southern plantation.[clxxxii]

On July 31, 1883, President Chester Arthur came to Louisville and proclaimed the Southern Exposition open to the public. The Art Gallery, which was located in Central Park, contained private collections from J. P. Morgan, August Belmont, Jay Gould, Victor Newcomb, former president of the Louisville & Nashville Railroad, and John Jacob Aster. The Smithsonian Institute furnished paintings and former President Ulysses Grant loaned a collection of curios, given to him during his travels around the world. Paul Phillipoteaux's ten foot by twenty foot painting of "*The French Revolution of 1848*" was the highlight of the collection. Robert Koehler and Thomas Eakins displayed their art. "*A Gainesboro Landscape*" and a "*Sunset*" by George Inness were also on loan from other museums.[clxxxiii]

By 8:30 pm., over five thousand people gathered to see the Exposition building and displays. People paid fifty cents to enter the Exposition to see the one hundred arch lights and the 1,800 incandescent lights, which lit up the building at night. The Exposition spent $107,220 dollars on musical entertainment. By 10:30 p.m. the Exposition closed their doors for the day. Over twenty thousand people attended the first day.[clxxxiv]

When the doors closed on November 1, 1883, over thirty thousand people attended the exhibition that day alone. During the one hundred days the Exposition ran, over 770,129 people attended the event, with an additional 200,933 admitted on passes.[clxxxv] To put the numbers into perspective, the amount of people who attended the Exposition exceeded over six times the city population, which at the time, was 123,762 people. The Exposition of 1883 exceeded anyone's expectations. The Southern Exposition of 1883 was the most profitable exhibition ever held and the exhibitors made money; for example, of the six hundred car loads of machinery from the Eastern states, less than one hundred car loads went back to the states, because the articles on exhibit were sold during the exhibition. The show was a perfect combination of North and South, Northern manufacturers brought manufactured and manufacturing articles that met the needs of the Southern market and the Southern market brought raw materials, such as cotton, coal, iron, trees, and field products for the Northern markets.

On November 12, 1883, Andrew Cowan wrote an article to the *Louisville Courier-Journal* entitled: *The Day After: A Walk through the Exposition Building Yesterday...*" In the article Cowan wrote that the exhibitors were finishing their packing, the fruit stands were empty, the popcorn man's effects had disappeared, and only a heap of broken paste board boxes showed where the soap and perfumery display had been. Very few of the exhibitors were left at the Exposition and the silence was broken by hammers and saws. "The Exposition was over!" was written everywhere.

As for the Art Gallery, all of the pictures that had been sold had been taken from the walls and were leaned against a long row of benches, placed in the center of the east gallery. The pictures on loan from the citizens of Louisville were gathered together and returned, and the pictures loaned from private collections in other cities were boxed and sent away.[clxxxvi]

Cowan posed the question, as did the rest of the board members, as to whether there should be another exposition. Cowan wrote: "It is useless to discuss the advantages which we have already enjoyed. Only the chronic grumbler and the man with a grievance, real or imaginary, will stop to argue the question. A year ago we had nothing but hope and fears. Today we have confidence, Exposition buildings, and machinery that cost over $300,000, and, besides, a reputation for success of more value than can be estimated."[clxxxvii] Cowan stated that the Southern states had not been properly represented in 1883. He also stated that the legislatures were not in session to make suitable appropriations for state exhibits. There was not enough time to enlist the support of individuals. He stated that the reputation of Louisville for enterprise had scarcely been asserted. He also stated that powerful rivals opposed the board's efforts and disputed every "inch of ground from the first step to the final and successful close."[clxxxviii]

He wrote that another Exposition would command and receive the support of the South. States such as Georgia, Mississippi, Louisiana, Texas, North and South Carolina, and Virginia could not afford and would not consent to being absent a second time, while Tennessee, Atlanta, Arkansas, Florida and Kentucky, represented in 1883, largely through private enterprise, would come with far more imposing and interesting representations of their undeveloped wealth. Southern manufacturing was absent from the 1883 Exposition and if they had another Exposition, they would not repeat the same mistake. In his open letter to the editor, Cowan wrote: "Louisville has been called slow, but is she not awake? The South has been slow to make known her advantages, to invite emigration, to invite capital, those mighty forces that have made the desert bloom and the rugged mountains yield their treasure. We have shaken their repose, and with two great industrial and mechanical expositions within her borders last year there will be such an awakening as may astonish the most enthusiastic believer in the South."[clxxxix]

Cowan wrote that the Southern Exposition should be about the South and that Kentucky's own future depended on the growth of the South. He stated that Louisville should keep the Southern Exposition alive for at least one more year. According to Cowan, the number and importance of the exhibits, the attendance of visitors from abroad, the art features and the music should be increased and improved another year. In order for the Exposition to occur in 1884, Cowan stated the board needed three things: First, the consent of the owners of the present site to lease or sell; second, the hearty, unqualified support of the people and press for the men who, sacrificing private interest and personal comfort may be induced to undertake the labor; and third, the money to pay the preliminary expenses. The running expenses for the Exposition for 100 days was $160,000, with receipts accounting $225,000, with a net profit of $65,000 over running expenses. The projectors asked for $300,000 capital, and hoped to secure the money, but the total amount paid in was less than $240,000. The plant cost about $315,000, leaving a debt of about $75,000 when the Exposition opened. The amount had been almost wholly paid so that the plant, which cost $315,000, would be nearly free of debt. Many of the Board of Directors and several merchants not on the Board, pledged their personal credit to raise the money to meet every obligation on demand. The Board was unanimously in support of another Exposition. But Cowan wrote there was no time to spare. "The merchants and manufacturers who realized the financial benefits of such an enterprise, the thousands who appreciated its advantages as an educational and refining power, the tens of thousands who had enjoyed the delightful music and the beautiful art treasures, fit for the palaces of kings, the whole people, in a word, who have enjoyed its varied attractions and shared its benefits, financial, educational, and social, should unite in a movement to secure another Exposition in 1884."[cxc]

The General Manager and stockholders held a meeting and decided to re-open the show and raised two hundred thousand dollars to buy the land. A new organization followed with Bennett Young as President of the Southern Exposition, J.H. Lindenberger, vice president, and N. Bloom as second vice president, John Green, Third Vice President, J. W. Stine as Fourth Vice President, Charles Pettett, Fifth Vice President, J. M. Wright as General Manager.[cxci]

The Board of Directors made a large change as the how many days the Exposition ran. No longer would the Exposition run one hundred days. The Exposition would open August 16 and close their doors on October 25. The Exposition began to make improvements and expanded their displays. The Exposition added more pictures in the Art Gallery, making the collection distinctly American. The collection made the Exposition one of the best collections in the West or South. The Exposition added several pieces of statuary made by the Kentucky sculptor Joel T. Hart, including his "Triumph of Chastity." In order for everyone to attend the Exposition, the Board of Directors decided to lower the admission on opening day from .50 cents to .25 cents. A visitor could purchase a season ticket for eight dollars for adults and five dollars for children under twelve years and under.[cxcii]

During the 1884 Southern Exposition, Andrew Cowan and his business partner Charles Mantle decided to set up a display of their company in the Southern Exposition building. The display showed their company's goods in oak tanned leather and leather belting and advertised they were dealers in foreign and domestic leather and mill supplies. Around the partition, which enclosed the exhibit space, were large hides, including sole leather, while hides were lighter and finished in black on one side. The exhibit of leather contained every type of example of leather from a bull's hide to the French kid. They also displayed tanner's tools, and materials, complete outfits for saddler's shops, for boot maker's and for all kinds of makers sewing machines, lasts, finished boots and shoes. The company also had an exhibit for H. W. John asbestos materials, including liquid paints, oils, roofing materials, packing for steam pipes, fire proof materials.[cxciii]

On May 21, 1884, the Polytechnic Art Gallery opened to the general public in Louisville. The gallery opened on the second floor of the Polytechnic building. Colonel Bennett Young was the president of the Polytechnic Society. Andrew Cowan was a member of the Art Committee and spoke at the opening. In his speech, he stated that he hoped that Louisville public spirited men would not only leave money for public enterprises when they died, but also during their lives aid in the establishment of art galleries, of libraries, of parks, and other public institutions. He hoped that Louisville citizens would raise $100,000 dollars to erect a building for the Polytechnic Society. He stated that the businessmen owed it to themselves to provide the young men of Louisville the means to be surrounded by the best influences. He stated that Louisville needed a library that was free to the public. The library should have an art gallery. He also stated that Louisville should have an industrial art school, for the young men that work in the factories.[cxciv]

The Southern Exposition continued to run from 1884 to 1887, and served as a catalyst for development in the surrounding area. In 1885, 260 homes valued at an average cost of $6,150, or $1.6 million dollars, were constructed between Kentucky and Magnolia Streets. After the Southern Exposition closed their doors in 1887, William Slaughter, president of the Victoria Land Company, bought the vacated property from the Southern Exposition. By 1887, the city began to guild over ten million dollars in construction contracts. The most popular Victorian style houses built were the Queen Anne and the Richardsonian Romanesque. On March 1887, the *Courier-Journal* declared Louisville the "New Gotham" and hailed that the city had the most beautiful homes. By 1887,

Louisville had ninety-four miles of street railways. Nineteen million people rode the street railways ever year. By 1890, Louisville had 161,129 residents, making the city twentieth in urban size in the United States. Louisville had grown to a stable manufacturing and commercial base. Louisville became the world's largest tobacco market. By the 1890's, Louisville had nineteen distilleries. Louisville was also the largest producer of cast iron pipe, made by Dennis Long & Company. The city also was the world's largest producer of plows, made by Avery & Company. Louisville also became the largest producers of jean cloth, producing eight million yards every year. The city also had sixteen tanneries with $2.5 million dollar in sales annually Louisville expanded in their woodworking industry and meat packing houses.[cxcv] Louisville lived up to the city's motto "The City of Progress." In 1890, the Exposition site was transformed into the Saint James Court and Belgravia development, which still stands today as a testament to the Southern Exposition's ideals of commerce and progress, Southern hospitality and Northern ingenuity.

The Statue of Liberty

In 1865, as the Civil War drew to a close, the French historian Edouard de Laboulaye proposed that France create a statue to give to the United States in celebration of America in building a viable democracy. The sculptor Frederic Auguste Bartholdi, known for his large scale sculptures, earned the commission. He would call his bronze statue "Liberty Enlightening the World." The goal was to have the statue completed in time of the centennial of the Declaration of Independence in 1876. The funding of the project would be a joint effort between the people of France and the United States. The French people would provide the funding for the statue and the assembly, and the United States would build the pedestal on which the statue would stand. The statue would be a symbol of friendship between France and the United States. France had a difficult time raising the funds needed for the statue, but helped raise the money by charging public fees, various forms of entertainment and a lottery.[cxcvi]

Bartholdi needed the assistance of an engineer to address the structural issues associated with designing such a massive copper structure. Alexandre Gustave Eiffel was commissioned to design the massive iron pylon and secondary skeletal framework, which allowed the statue's copper skin to move independently yet stand upright. Work on the sculpture did not begin until 1875.[cxcvii]

In America, fundraising efforts to build the pedestal also went slowly, so Joseph Pulitzer, who was the editor of *The World*, used his paper to raise the funds. Pulitzer criticized the rich who failed to finance the pedestal construction and the middle class who were content to rely upon the wealthy to provide the funds. The campaign worked. Fundraising efforts for the pedestal also included contests, benefits, and exhibitions.[cxcviii]

The statue would be placed upon a granite pedestal inside the courtyard of the star-shaped walls of Fort Wood, which was built during the War of 1812 and located on Bedloe's Island, off the southern tip of Manhattan in upper New York Bay. The name of each state of the Union was to be engraved on the pedestal. The pedestal was designed by American architect Richard Morris Hunt, and the chief engineer for the construction of the pedestal was Charles P. Stone. The cost of the statue was $250,000 and a campaign to raise another $250,000 was being raised to pay of the pedestal.[cxcix]

By November 30, 1883, only $100,000 had been raised. The committee in charge of the statue asked the American people to raise the rest of the money. Charles Jacob, the mayor of Louisville, along with Andrew Cowan, Walter Halderman, Samuel Churchill, Bidermann DuPont, Isaac Caldwell, C.E. Sears, and R.M. Kelly formed a committee to help raise money for the pedestal. The committee asked all the different social and benevolent orders and societies and the religious associations throughout the state to unite in the effort to give Kentucky a noticeable place upon the pedestal. They did not ask for large contributions, and the smallest sum would be received. They desired that the money raised was to be through small contributions from a large amount of people and the names of the people subscribing was to be written down and forwarded with the sums to Charles Jacob, the chairman of the Committee, who would send them to William Maxwell Evarts, who was the chairman of the American Committee for the Statue of Liberty.[cc]

In 1885, the Statue of Liberty was completed, disassembled, and packed into more than two hundred crates and shipped to New York. The statue arrived in New York in June of 1885. For four months, workers re-assembled the Statue of Liberty and mounted the statue on the pedestal. The height of the statue with the pedestal reached 305 feet. On October 28, 1886, President Grover Cleveland officially dedicated the Statue of Liberty.[cci]

Chapter 13

Founding of the Louisville Park System

In 1880, Baxter Square Park was purchased by the city of Louisville to become the city's first park. In 1888, Mayor Charles Jacob purchased Burnt Knob, named Jacob Park. With the start of the first park, Cowan prepared a paper to the Salmagundi Club, of which he was a member, on the importance of parks. In his paper, he outlined a plan for the establishment of a park system for Louisville and offered to furnish copies of the park acts of every city where public parks had been established if the Salmagundi Club would undertake to put the plan before the public.[ccii] The Salmagundi Club was a society organization that advocated mutual improvement. In their meetings they asked questions and discussed topics in philosophy, science, art, history biography, literature, political, and social economy. The question provoked the Salmagundi Club to form a committee for a parks system to write a report. Andrew Cowan wrote down the report.[cciii]

On June 5, 1887, the *Louisville Courier-Journal* published a commentary that literally changed the landscape of Louisville. Some of the most prominent businessmen in Louisville, such as Andrew Cowan, William J. Davie, ex-Confederate John E. Green, S.E. Jones, Charles Hermany, J.H. Lindenberger, C.W. Kelly, A.R. Cooper, ex-Confederate General Basil Duke, Edgar Hounsfield, A.P. Humphrey, R.W. Knotts, Thomas Speed, J.M. Wright, ex-Confederate Bennett Young, William R. Belknap, John Mason Brown, George M. Davis, Harry Weissinger, Rufus Saxton, and Henry Watterson, wrote a report advocating a park system in Louisville and submitted the report to the *Louisville Courier-Journal.*[cciv]

The report stated four reasons why the city should have a parks system. The first reason was to enhance the city's status. Civic leaders no longer wanted to be viewed as second rate. The second reason stated that the public parks would be for the recreation and health of

Louisville residents. The largest part of Louisville residents had no advantages to escape the heat during the summer months in their small dwellings in the city. According to the report, hundreds of Louisville residents died because they lacked pure air and "wholesome recreation." The third reason stated that the parks would attract businesses, and additional commerce would translate into more tax revenues. The fourth reason for a parks system would lead to increased property values. Higher residential costs would translate into more tax revenues.[ccv]

The report lined out three large parks. East Park was located next to the Ohio River near Zorn Avenue. The West Park would also be adjacent to the Ohio River at the western terminus of Broadway. The South Park was to be located at the southern end of Fourth Street, and parkways would interconnect all three parks. Mayor Charles Jacob, who was independently wealthy, helped support the Salmagundi Club's efforts for a park system. He used his own money to facilitate the park's implementation.[ccvi]

The Park Act was written by Cowan and John Mason Brown at the request of the Commercial Club. Cowan was active in securing the passage of the Parks Act by the legislature and adoption by the people at a special election. He was one of the first elected park commissioners, and was elected a member of the first Board of Park commissioners for three years, during which time the park lands were purchased and their development entrusted to Frederick Law Olmstead.

Olmstead was considered the greatest park architect in the country at the time. He was born in 1822 in Connecticut and acquired his love for scenic vistas and outdoor skills from his father, John Olmstead, who took the young Frederick on excursions in the rural countryside. John Olmstead read Humphrey Repton and J.C. Loudon, who were authorities in landscape. When Frederick began to design parks, he worked hard to provide opportunities for city people to experience the beauty, grandeur, and impressiveness and benefits of parks. The core of his philosophy was the experience of nature should be available to all people, contact with nature has the power to soothe human souls and promote health, and experiencing nature's beauty promotes moral perception and intuition. The newly formed Park Board invited Olmstead to come to Louisville to review their ideas for a park system.

On May 20, 1891, Olmstead arrived in Louisville. By 1891, Olmstead had already been practicing landscape architecture for thirty-four years. Olmstead's report to the commissioners analyzed the unique natural characteristics of each park and recommended that each should be designed to reflect the unique character of each site. Shawnee Park would provide riverside expanse suited to accommodate crowds of people brought together for activities and entertainments on broad areas of lawn, in picnic groves, and around flower gardens. The terraced landscape would reach to the river's edge, and would be created through the eventual planting of trees. Cherokee park focused on interior landscape of changing ridgelines to stream valleys. Iroquois Park was to be a scenic reservation of forests, savannahs, and summit views, surrounded by countryside.[ccvii]

In 1893, Cowan ran for reelection as park commissioner. During the election, he ran as an independent candidate. He could not accept the nomination for the Republican Party, because, as he stated "like hundreds of Democrats, and Republicans, I contended for a strictly business management of the parks, and opposed to having the new department of the city government become a mero screw in the political machine."[ccviii] Hoping to rally public support for his reelection, Cowan wrote in the *Louisville Courier-Journal* that the first year of the board was to plan and organize the work for the parks system, within the restrictions of the park law, which was accomplished. The land for East Park (or Cherokee Park) was bought for three hundred dollars an acre. Cowan was able to obtain 305 acres for Cherokee park. Next, the deeds to Southern Parkway or the Grand Boulevard from South Louisville to Iroquois Park were secured. The cost of Southern Parkway was $91,000. The South park property was surveyed and the commissioners bought 240 acres of additional land, making Iroquois park 350 acres. Total cost for Iroquois park was $90,800. Two electric car lines ran out of Iroquois park, and both were built in two years. Boone Square was purchased at a cost of $37,000. The two market house spaces on Market Street, known and Logan place and Kenton place, were transformed into breathing spaces and playgrounds for children with a cost of $7,500. The Western park was purchased. The park extended from the Ohio River, extending from Broadway north to Walnut Street, which would become Shawnee Park. Cowan hoped that Shawnee would be the gem of the parks system. Shawnee was 169 acres and the total cost was $126,000. Cowan was proud of the accomplishments of completing his anchor parks, Iroquois, Cherokee and Shawnee.

Olmstead and his firm eventually designed sixteen parks and three parkways for the Louisville park system, including Central Park, Baxter Square, Chickasaw Park, Algonquin Park, Seneca Park, Churchill Park, Bingham Park, Elliott Square, Shelby Park, Tyler Park, Victory Park, Wayside Park, Boone Square, William Stansbury Park, Willow Park.[ccix]

In 1893, Cowan was defeated in the reelection for Park Commissioner as an independent candidate, but upon impeachment of Frederick Gibbs, against his will, Cowan was chosen by the new board to fill the vacancy on November 28, 1894.[ccx] At the end of his second term, he was nominated by his political party for the same office but declined the nomination. He was reelected in 1907 on a fusion ticket and served for one year as President of the Board. In November of 1908, he stepped down as commissioner because he had moved to a new home beyond the city limits. A commissioner could only be elected if he lived in the city.[ccxi]

Today's Louisville park system would far exceed Cowan's vision. The Louisville and Jefferson county park systems is one of the oldest in the nation and Cowan's original parks system of Cherokee, Iroquois, and Shawnee has expanded to one hundred and twelve parks with more than eleven thousand acres of parkland and fifteen miles of historic parkways.[ccxii]

The Board of Park Commissioners continued to add neighborhood parks, interior squares and local playgrounds. In 1938, the Iroquois Amphitheater was built at Iroquois Park by the Works Projects Administration. In 1942, the board of commissioners was replaced with the Department of Parks and Recreation and in 1944 the Jefferson County Fiscal Court created a Playground and Recreation Board for the administration of properties outside the city. In 1946, the Jefferson Memorial Forest initial tracts of land were acquired by the city. In 1947, Otter Creek Park in Brandenburg, Kentucky was given to the city of Louisville by the Federal government and Highview Park was also acquired. In 1956, the City Parks and Recreation Department continued to buy land and buy Cox Park in in 1952, Chenoweth, now Vettiner, and Hounz Lane and Long Run Park. In 1961, the city bought McNeely Park. In 1964, Waverly Park was acquired by the Department.

In 1968, the recreation and park management functions for the city and county were merged to become the Metropolitan Parks and Recreation Board or simply known as Metro Parks. The County acquired 3,338 acres of land, including 1,721 in the Memorial Forest, supervised playgrounds, swimming pools, community buildings, golf courses, camping areas, and cultural arts centers. The City acquired 2,211 acres of land as well as eleven community centers, playgrounds, swimming pools, and golf courses. In 1986, the management of the properties was turned over to the Louisville and Jefferson County Parks Department. In 1989, the Louisville Olmstead Parks Conservatory was created. By 1998, the Metro Parks system managed 112 parks, 12,600 acres, nine golf courses, 14 swimming pools, and 19 community centers. In 2000, the Southwest Community Center opened in Louisville. In 2001, the 56-acre Thurman Hutchins Park opened to the public. In 2002, the Louisville Extreme Park and 130-acre Miles Park opened to the public. Fairmount Falls Park was acquired by the city. In 2004 Locust Grove and Riverside-The Farnsley-Moremen Landing became part of the Metro Parks system. In 2005, the Jefferson County Memorial Park expanded to 6,000 acres. By 2012, Metro Parks included 122 park covering more than 13,000 acres, with nine golf courses, 16 community centers, five swimming pools, two historic homes, and the nation's largest municipal urban forest. The park system of today now has fishing lakes, two public riding stables, archery ranges, hiking trails, bridle trails, and team building courses.[ccxiii] The latest project for the Metro Parks system is to interconnect all the parks with a bike trail and the addition of Waterfront Park.

Cowan's dream of a Louisville park system has far exceeded his expectations. Although most people think that Olmstead was the founder of the idea for the Louisville Park System, Andrew Cowan was the gentleman who presented the idea before the members of the Salmagundi Club and the Commercial Club. If you go to Iroquois Park, Cherokee Park, or Shawnee Park, you will find no monuments, no markers, or any tributes to Andrew Cowan for his vision of building the three parks and being the first elected park commissioner.

Chapter 14

The Blue and Gray Reunion at Gettysburg: 1887

On July 3, 1886, at Gettysburg, Pennsylvania, Cowan's New York Battery held a reunion and selected a site for a monument to the 1st New York Independent Battery.[ccxiv] A year later, on July 3, 1887, the Union and Confederate soldiers met at the Gettysburg battlefield. At 1:30 p.m., the procession formed at the Eagle Hotel, and followed by the band, took up the march toward the place where the Philadelphia Union soldiers had held their position against Confederate General George Pickett's charge. The procession proceeded out Baltimore Street to the place where the Emmittsburg Road joined it, and was the outer post of the Union sharpshooters during the fight. Out the Emmittsburg Road to the battlefield avenue, the wearers of blue badges and white helmets proceeded to the "Bloody Angle" and the band began to play "Rally 'Round the Flag, Boys." The Philadelphia procession reached the stone wall and the monuments that were being erected to the 69th and 71st Pennsylvania Infantry.[ccxv]

At 2:00 p.m., the 69th Pennsylvania veterans marched to the stand erected for speeches. The names of the killed and wounded of the 69th Pennsylvania were read aloud. Union General Joshua Owen delivered the oration. During his speech, he stated that he hardly knew what to say to the men who twenty-four years before emerged from the woods 1,300 yards away and made the terrible assault on the Union line. He told the gathered crowd: "Let them place their monument where they wish. Armistead and several others pierced our line and here within a few feet of this spot he fell, wounded unto death. The renowned phalanxes of Alexander would have not dared to make the charge Pickett's division made."[ccxvi] In closing, he called for three cheers for Pickett's division as proof of his friendship. The monument was then dedicated.

Before the ceremonies had begun, Mrs. LaSalle Corbell Pickett was seated on the platform and the crowded cheered as she took her seat. The 71st Pennsylvania Infantry was the next monument to be dedicated and Union General William Burns, who took over for General Laurence Baker in command, gave his speech. He stated that Pickett's charge would live in song and its sad requiem would echo the Philadelphia brigade. He stated the Philadelphia brigade fraternizes with Pickett's division. Both sides recognized each other's bravery and respected each other's fame. "The world will applaud both alike, and history will record their deeds together."[ccxvii]

Union Colonel R. Penn Smith, of the 71st Pennsylvania, presented the monument erected by his regiment in honor of Lt. Alonzo Cushing and the 4th United States Artillery. After Smith gave his speech, the crowd moved to the clump of trees where Cowan's battery monument was erected. Colonel Andrew Cowan introduced Reverend James K. Dixon, who offered a prayer. Mrs. Pickett walked up the platform. Colonel Cowan rose from his seat and thanked Mrs. Pickett for her presence and also welcomed the wife of the commander of the Philadelphia brigade, who was during the battle, an aide to General Alexander Webb's staff, who brought Cowan the orders to move his guns to where the monument to Cowan's battery was erected. Cowan introduced Serino E. Payne. After Payne gave his speech, Cowan transferred the monument to the Gettysburg Memorial Association. Lieutenant William Sawyers, on behalf of the battery, thanked Cowan for his efforts to bring about the dedication and making the dedication a success.[ccxviii] The 1st New York Independent Battery monument has the inscription "Double Canister At Ten Yards, July 3, 1863, Cowan's First New York Battery, Artillery Brigade, Sixth Corps" on the front and on the rear of the monument has inscribed: "Erected in memory of our comrades, July 3, 1887. The World Can Never Forget What They Did Here.'"

According to the newspaper account, the most interesting incident of the whole dedication was the presentation by Cowan to the Pickett's Division Association of a sword that he took during Pickett's charge. The sword was three feet long; the handle was of mother of pearl, and the blade of finely polished steel. During Pickett's charge a young rebel officer jumped toward the gun at which he was standing, but was immediately shot down and his sword fell at Cowan's feet. Cowan kept the sword but was never able to return the sword to the rebel soldier's family. He hoped that the Pickett's Division Association would be able to return the sword the family. Confederate Major J.C. Crocker, of Virginia, accepted the sword and promised to try and find the family. Cowan introduced General William Smith and General Hunt to the assembly. After the men were introduced, the crowd dispersed and went back into town. During the night, the old veterans slept in over one hundred tents on the battlefield, with four hospital tents for the very frail veterans.[ccxix]

Chapter 15

The Grand Army of the Republic Reunion: 1895

In September of 1895, the national membership of the Grand Army of the Republic met in Louisville for their 29th annual Grand Encampment. For two years, the city's leaders planned for the event. The theme of the encampment was to be reconciliation between the North and South, since this was the first encampment held below the Mason-Dixon Line. Dignitaries from both sides were to attend the event.[ccxx] Resources in Louisville were pulled together to meet the needs and demands of the 150,000 Union Civil War veterans for the reunion. Individuals, organizations and entrepreneurs, both public and private, official and informal, legitimate and illicit, prepared for the city's first big national assembly. The reunion would be held between September 4 through 15, 1895.[ccxxi]

The city would have to feed, house, transport and entertain the thousands of conventioneers. *The New York Times* reported that 150 coaches brought forty-four thousand people to Louisville for the convention and the railroads were pushed to their limit with the unprecedented number of visitors to the city. *The New York Times* reported that the attendance was one of the largest in the history of the G.A.R.[ccxxii] The Naval Veterans Association took command of the of the boats *William Tell* and *Carrie Hope* and the official fleet was placed in commission with the usual naval exercises. The ex-sailors were welcome by Kentucky Governor John Y. Brown and Mayor Henry Tyler. Every benevolent, civic and business club or society became involved in the massive undertaking. Volunteers were recruited from the ranks of the G.A.R. membership and from women's auxiliaries in Louisville and nearby towns. The Louisville Legion and the Commerce Club were prominent members in volunteering to help the veterans during the convention. Veterans could stay at Encampment Tent City, "Camp Caldwell," a complex to house three thousand veterans in three hundred tents covering fifty acres. Schools were closed and the furniture removed to help with housing the veterans. The Louisville Street Car Company reconstructed its entire system to concentrate cars on lines serving major convention activity sites.[ccxxiii]

The convention's agenda included the election of officers and consideration of bonuses, pensions, holidays, and the next reunion location. After the business affairs of the day were over, the veterans had a program full of official events and secondary activities. Park concerts, as well as daily musicales and nightly campfires, were available. Fountaine Ferry, which was Louisville's largest entertainment park, remained opened for twenty-four hours. Racing and trotting tracks ran. Veterans were given tours of various manufactories. The Grand Opera House performed "Shenandoah," the vaudevillians played at the Buckingham Theater, and minstrel players performed at the Macauley Theater. Confederate General John Gordon read his "The Dark Days of the Confederacy" speech and Henry Watterson, the editor of the *Louisville Courier-Journal*, who served in the Confederacy, gave his "Abraham Lincoln" address.[ccxxiv]

The three major events for the G.A.R. reunion were the Grand Parade on Wednesday, Thursday's waterfront fireworks display and the all day picnic Friday. The Grand Parade, anticipated as a monumental tribute to the Grand Army's service, consisted of the Army's former military units, with an estimated thirty thousand participants. With forty-four guns, the column moved out on a winding course through downtown streets, ending at Phoenix Hill Park. Just before sunrise on the parade morning, two cannon crews of Battery A, 1st Regiment of the Kentucky State Guard, known as the Louisville Legion, left the downtown Louisville armory to Phoenix Hill Park. Cannon crews were to fire a forty-four gun salute at sunrise to awaken the city. Each cannon was to fire twenty-two times. When the second caisson, which was fifteen minutes behind the first, reached 4th and Broadway, at 5:30 a.m., an explosion occurred. Forty-four bags of black powder, each weighing 1.6 pounds, mysteriously ignited. The resulting explosion killed Corporal Arthur Langan Robinson, Private Charles Brechner, Private Charles C. Woods, Private Archibald McBride, and William Adams, Sr., an African American civilian driver. Sergeant Fred Conn and Private E.M. Hobbs received cuts and bruises and severe powder burns. Captain David Castleman, the officer in charge, was lifted fifteen feet off his horse, but escaped injury.[ccxxv] On September 13, the bodies of the soldiers were taken to the armory where they laid in state until 3:00 p.m. Twenty-four pallbearers from Battery A proceeded to Christ Church Cathedral for a joint funeral at 4:00 p.m. After the funeral, the bodies were laid to rest at Cave Hill Cemetery in Section O, Lot 44, grave numbers 3, 4, 5, 6, with full military honors.[ccxxvi]

Thursday's fireworks show had a viewing area stretching for ten blocks on the waterfront. When four thousand spectators gathered on the stands the eastern section collapsed, injuring thirty people. Many of the injured suffered broken legs, crushed feet, shoulders dislocated and sprang ankles.[ccxxvii]

Friday's primary event, the grand scale picnic, was held at Wilder Park. Over one hundred thousand people attended the event. One hundred cattle, three hundred sheep, and two hundred shoats were prepared for the barbeque, while fifteen kettles were needed for seventy-five gallons of burgoo. The burgoo and the "Old Plantation Cake Walk" tried to give the veterans a taste of what Louisville life was like. Although never confirmed, a rumor circulated that widespread food poisoning resulted from the picnic.[ccxxviii]

During the G.A.R. reunion, Andrew Cowan was Vice President of the Citizens Committee. As the veterans arrived in Louisville, many of his old comrades arrived in the city. On September 8, Cowan went to the Seventh Street Depot to meet some of his old comrades whom he had not seen in years. Dr. and Mrs. F.N. Walker; William Webster; Jason Crouch; Isaac Winter; Reid Johnson, his daughter and four ladies; David Nettleton; Lucius Goodyers; George Chidsy and Frederick Cossum all disembarked from the train. The train had come from Cayuga, New York. Before Cowan had finished shaking hands with them all, they seized him and pinned on his breast jacket a gold badge as a token of their appreciation. Cowan was touched by the remembrance. The badge consisted of a pair of cannons crossed at the top. Then followed eight gold bars, indicative of the positions filled by Colonel Cowan before he attained the rank of Chief of the Corps. On the lowest bar was inscribed the word "Private" then followed by "Corporal", then "Sergeant" then "Lieutenant" then "Captain" then "Major" and finally "Lieutenant Colonel." The topmost bar bore the inscription "Chief of Corps." Hanging from the bottom bar was a gold medal, set with a large diamond, upon which were painted the colors of the battery, which Colonel Cowan commanded. On the back of the badge was the inscription: "Col. Andrew Cowan, Louisville, Ky., September, 1895. From his comrades of the First New York Battery."[ccxxix]

The next day on September 10, Mrs. Emily E. Woodley, Past President of the Army Nurses, brought on a train a young tree from Pennsylvania wrapped in an American flag and with the tree came a can of earth from Independence Square, where the Declaration of Independence was signed. The "tree of peace" was to be planted in Eastern Park, at Shadyside. The first carriage to arrive for the ceremonies contained Confederate Colonel John B. Castleman, Mrs. John A. Logan, the wife of the Union General, Mrs. W.R. Belknap, and Mrs. L.A. Turner. The second carriage arrived and Lieutenant Colonel Morris Belknap, Mrs. Henry S. Tyler, President of the Ladies Committee, Mrs. Nettie Gunlock, President of the Ladies of the G.A.R., and Mrs. Simon B. Buckner, the wife of the Confederate General, departed from carriage. The last carriage brought Colonel Cowan and Mrs. Emma Wallace, after which seventy-five other people arrived at the location.[ccxxx]

The dirt from Independence Square was put in the hole and then a yew oak tree was planted in the hole. Mrs. Woodley gave a speech, followed by John Castleman, who was an officer in the Confederate army and Col. Cowan, who approached the tree and reaching above it shook hands and each declared that any feeling that might have existed between the North and South had been totally obliterated and that they formally declared that the Civil War was over. They were cheered by the women.[ccxxxi]

Mrs. Woodley gave the certificate certifying that the tree commemorated the 29th Encampment of the G.A.R. and in memory of Andrew G. Curtin, the War Governor of Pennsylvania, who called into service the Philadelphia Women's Nurse Corps No. 1, on May 23, 1861, who served until 1865, and honorably discharged. Emily Woodley was the last survivor.

In the evening on September 10, Andrew Cowan gave a banquet for the G.A.R. Commander in Chief Lawler and his staff, General T.N. Walker of Indianapolis, the leading candidate to succeed Lawler, ex-Speaker Warren Kiefer of Ohio, Colonel J.M. Schoonmaker, and Henry Watterson. According to *The Louisville Courier-Journal*, the banquet was one of the most elegant private affairs that had ever been given in Louisville. The interior and exterior of his home was a "fairyland." The front of the house was lit with many colored lanterns, which were hung from the roof to the foundation and sent streams of light all along the avenue. The hall and reception rooms were draped in festoons of red, white and blue bunting and cut flowers enhanced the scene. In dining room the decorations were notable for their design and elaborateness. The guests were seated at a large mahogany table, and the tablecloth was made from a rich white damask cloth that served as a foundation for the national colors, which were woven into the cloth. In the center was a tall cut glass Venetian vase containing white roses. About the vase was tied a bowknot of red, white and blue ribbon. At either end of the table were cut glass candelabras, with white shades and small flags attached. Two large floral designs were placed on the table. One was a Union shield with G.A.R. and the other was a Maltese Cross, which was the badge for the Sixth Corps. The candelabra shades also had red, white and blue ribbon. A ten course meal was served to the guests. The cakes were molded into small flags. The guest cards were hand painted and designed with the heads of American girls painted with Army insignia.[ccxxxii]

On September 11, G.A.R. veterans met at a huge campfire held at the National Park. The band from the Soldier's Home of Marion, Indiana led by Captain John Stalk, gave a concert. At 8:00 p.m., Captain John Fowler, Chairman in charge of the event, called the meeting in order and introduced Confederate Captain John H. Leathers, who acted as presiding officer of the evening.

Captain Leathers mentioned that he was a member of Confederate General Stonewall Jackson's brigade and a former member of the C.S.A., but now belonged to the U.S.A. Captain Leathers was greeted with applause. He declared the campfire opened by announcing the Hayden Quartet. The Quartet sang "His Young Love" and 'Tick Tack", which was followed by Seally's band and more speaking and music followed.[ccxxxiii]

Colonel Cowan was the first speaker of the evening. He made a short speech welcoming the Grand Army to the city. He assured the veterans that the citizens of Louisville appreciated their visit, and that everything would be done to secure their comfort and pleasure while in the city. He told the crowd that the day before was the proudest day in his life since Lee surrendered at Appomattox and that the citizens of Louisville welcomed their honored guests. In his closing, he stated that the day before was the greatest day Louisville had ever seen and the people of the city were glad that the G.A.R. was in the city.

Captain John Leathers gave a speech expressing his devotion to the country, saying that "we are all a united people, North and South, living in one country and under one flag, and that the passion engendered by the war was rapidly passing away." He was cheered again and again by the crowd during his speech.

Besides the speeches, Mr. Charles Gordon rendered a trombone solo, Master Willie Hart recited a piece called "Soldier's Joys," Master Clifford Grapes gave an exhibition drill, and sang "Marching Through Georgia." The New Albany Drill Corps, comprised of sixteen young women, gave a flag drill. The "original soldier-boy of the Rappahannock" Robert Henry Hendershot, accompanied by a flute, gave a number of selections that received several encores. Although middle aged, he still handled his drumsticks with as much energy as he did when he was a drummer boy in the Union army. The evening was brought to end when the men sang "Doxology"

When the G.A.R. convention finally came to a close, the Citizens Committee gave a final report. Cowan stated that during the week's activities he served sandwiches, lemonade and cigars all day and endeavored to make the veterans feel at home. The rate of one penny per mile each way over all the railroads in the United States to Louisville would pay for the wholesale merchants for all they contributed for the expense of entertaining the encampment. The retail trade of the city, most railway lines, and the hotels and restaurants, saloons, etc., did a thriving business and were well rewarded. Cowan stated that the chief and lasting advantage to be derived from the city would come from advertising of the advantages and the city's generous treatment of the veterans. A hundred thousand guests praised Louisville. The veterans learned that the citizens of Louisville were loyal and good, and that they were respectable and substantial representatives of the American people. He admitted that the fireworks show was poor, but he pointed out that the show was not the fault of the Executive Council, who contracted for the finest display that Pain could propose, and agreed to his price. The reception given to the officers and delegates at the Auditorium surpassed anything that Cowan had seen in the way of social entertainments. Cowan felt that the visitors have "gone away delighted and charmed. The people here are better for the lesson taught by the meeting of the Grand Army on Southern soil and an influence has gone forth that will be of lasting benefit to the whole country. Could ask for more?"[cxxxiv]

Chapter 16

The Confederate Veterans Reunion: 1905

On April 15, 1896, the Kentucky Institute for the Blind elected Andrew Cowan as the president of its board of directors. On June 2, 1900, Andrew Cowan hold a reception for Mrs. LaSalle Corbell Picket, the wife of Confederate General George Pickett. Confederate General George Picket had died in 1875. Over five hundred guests had the opportunity to meet Mrs. Pickett. Normally Mrs. Pickett wore the traditional gray, but for Cowan's reception, she wore Union blue. When some of the Virginians noticed her in the Union blue, they asked her why she wore the blue dress. She explained that she wore the blue gown as a compliment to her host, whose "valorous deeds at Gettysburg" were known to the Confederates, and when she had finished her impromptu speech, three cheers were given for Cowan.[ccxxxv]

The flag of the 18th Virginia Infantry, torn and tattered, was draped in the drawing room in back of Colonel Cowan and Mrs. Cowan, and Mrs. Pickett and became the subject of comment during the reception. The hall was fragrant with white lilies and red flox, and several magnolias formed a frame about a large engraving of the Battle of Gettysburg. The drawing room was arranged with red and white roses and the library was a mass of rose-pink peonies and white carnations. At the reception was ex-Confederate General and ex-Kentucky governor Simon Bolivar Buckner, former Kentucky governor Luke Blackburn, William Belknap, William Cheatham, S.A. Culbertson, ex-Confederate General Basil Duke, R.W. Knott, Lunsford Yandell, Albert Cowan, and Charles Pettet.[ccxxxvi]

In June of 1905, the Confederate Veterans held their fifteenth reunion in Louisville, Kentucky. The first meeting to arrange for the reunion was held on October 27, 1904, at the home of Colonel Bennett Young. Captain John Leathers, commander of the George Eastin Camp, Confederate Veterans, presided over the meeting and read an outline of what was to be done. Early in 1905, permanent headquarters were set up at Fourth and Chestnut streets in the Presbyterian Church. President of the Committee was John Leathers, who was manager of the Louisville National Banking Company. Bennett Young was the vice president and owned a large legal business. General John B. Castleman was in charge of the invitations. General Basil Duke managed the transportation affairs. Cowan was the chairman of the Committee on Entertainment of the General Officers for the Confederate reunion in Louisville. Cowan held the reception for the Confederate officers at The Pendennis Club. During the reception, twenty-five Confederate officers surrounded Cowan and presented him with a loving cup in recognition of their high esteem for him personally and for the services he had given to help the committee entertain their comrades during the Confederate reunion. The cup was made of silver and the handles made from deer horns.

The presentation was made by members of the George Eastin Camp, United Confederate Veterans, including John Leathers, John Pirtle, Abner Harris, Thomas Bullitt, John Weller, Bennett Young, John Green, John B. Castleman, Basil Duke, John Gathright, Thomas Osborne, Elijah Basye, Samuel Buchanan, George Norton, Dosier Thornton, Theodore Burnett, J.G. Minnigerode, Randolph Blain, David Sanders, A.E. Richards, Walter B. Halderman, W.A. Milton, W.O. Harris, Harry Weissinger, R.C. Davis, Henry Stone, Emmet Field, John S. Jackman, and H.A. Witherspoon.

General Duke took the cup and gave a short speech. In his speech, he stated that the loving cup was presented to Cowan, as the inscription recites, by his Confederate friends of Louisville as a memento of the kindly assistance he rendered them in entertaining their comrades and guests of the reunion. He continued in his speech that the cup was given as a slight token of their appreciation of the liberal sentiments he had ever evinced, and the substantial aid he had never failed to contribute in every matter, social or benevolent, in which the Confederates of Louisville had been concerned, and because they wish to show, in some conspicuous way that they recognize and were grateful for his generous friendship and sympathy.[ccxxxvii]

Duke stated that the cup was also intended as a testimonial of respect and admiration from soldiers to a "true and gallant soldier," from men who proud of their courage and constancy exhibited in the ranks where they served, were yet prompt to acknowledge the valor and prowess of those who fought against them, and who they only believe could have overcome them. Duke stated that the knowing Cowan's "record, military and civil, so well as we do, how as commanded by the picked soldiery of the Empire State, you turned the tide at Gettysburg, and served with distinction on many other fields, and how in civil life your best efforts have been constantly devoted to the welfare of our city, we know that in honoring you, we render recognition to the best type of the American soldier and to those qualities which we admire most in a gentleman and a fellow citizen."[ccxxxviii]

After Duke's speech, Colonel Cowan arose and gave a speech. He thanked the Confederate veterans and stated that he was fortunate enough to serve with the Army of the Potomac throughout the Civil War. In his speech he stated that the Army of Northern Virginia confronted the Army of the Potomac from the Chickahominy, from the Rappahannock to the Susquehanna, from the Rapidan to the Appomattox, with courage that never flinched, a "determination that was never broken, a devotion that no sacrifice, no privation, no danger could chill."[ccxxxix] He stated that when the Army of the Potomac finally looked on the remnant of the Army of Northern Virginia at Appomattox, and saw the end had come, no one could describe the Union soldier's feelings. General Ulysses S. Grant left the Confederate soldiers with their horses, but "I tell you they could have shared all we possessed, although most of it was on our backs and under our saddles, for the war left us poor, save for youth and courage. No one among them all got less than kind words and good wishes from the lowest to the biggest in our ranks. Let us remember that today, and tell the story to your children, for I know it is true."[ccxl]

Cowan went on to state in his speech that the Confederate and Union soldiers came through the great and bloody war with mutual respect. They both fought for what they believed was right. "The soldiers from both sides were not called upon to apologize for their actions, but if they were to answer, both sides would be quick and defiant. But, today both sides stand united and loyal under the Union flag. Should any man, or other men, at home or abroad, assail the flag, they would meet the sword and the world would see that the men of the South and North, the followers of Confederate General Robert E. Lee and of General Grant have instilled in their children the qualities of patriotism and courage that were tested and strengthened during the Civil War.[ccxli]

Cowan went on to say that he had lived in Louisville for thirty-nine years and had lived among "gallant men that wore the gray and my comrades of the blue, with ever growing respect and friendship between us." He stated that nothing he could do would ever repay the kindness and good will shown to him by the soldiers of both sides.

During his speech, Cowan stated the Confederates of Louisville welcomed the Grand Army of the Republic and the men in blue tried to show their appreciation for their hospitality and good will when the United Confederate Veterans met in Louisville five years earlier in 1897. At the end of his speech he asked the members who presented him his cup to help him christen the cup, which would be handed down as "a memento of one of the happiest occasions of my life." The cup was filled with champagne and Colonel Cowan first drank to the health and prosperity of all present. He passed the cup in turn to Judge Burnett, then he gave the cup to the other members as they drank to the health of Cowan. After the ceremony, the men sat down to a buffet lunch.

During the reunion, on June 14, Cowan was seen on the streets of Louisville wearing a suit of Confederate gray and was taken by hundreds for some Southern colonel of distinction. The *Louisville-Courier Journal* stated that Cowan "has always been recognized as one of Louisville's most progressive citizens, gifted with that spirit which enables any man to forgive and forget animosities."[ccxlii]

Chapter 17

The Abraham Lincoln Memorial at Hodgenville, Kentucky

As Lincoln's centennial approached, Richard Lloyd Jones, editor of the nationally circulated *Collier's Weekly* magazine, organized The Lincoln Farm Association. With donations from the social elite to school children, the Association raised money to purchase Lincoln's birth site at Sinking Springs Farm in Hodgenville, Kentucky. The Association also raised money to build a permanent memorial to Lincoln. In 1904 fundraising began for the project. By February 1909, the Lincoln Farm Association planned a huge celebration for the memorial event.[ccxliii] On February 8, Kentucky Governor Augustus Willison appointed General Roger Williams of Lexington as the chief marshal for the Lincoln centenary celebration at Hodgenville for February 12, 1909, on Lincoln's birthday. Williams had a conference with Cowan, who was chairman of the Lincoln Committee and would go to Hodgenville to make his arrangements. General Williams was to have charge of the organizations, both military and civilian. All organizations would report to Williams when they arrived at Hodgenville. General Williams also directed the march and would make sure there was no confusion at the Lincoln site. President Theodore Roosevelt was also to attend the memorial and lay the cornerstone for the memorial building.[ccxliv]

Also in attendance at the Lincoln celebration was the 1st Regiment of the Kentucky State Guard, also known as the Louisville Legion. One regiment for the Legion was to escort President Roosevelt. The soldiers would be an addition to the mounted infantry already assigned duty and would go on foot in full regalia. General P.P. Johnston ordered additional troops. Lieutenant Colonel James Gregory was in charge of all the troops and would select the company from the First Regiment that was to go on duty at the Lincoln farm. The first lady of Kentucky, Mrs.

Willison, was to also attend the event and accompany Mrs. Roosevelt. A band of twenty-two pieces was to play during the ceremonies at the Lincoln farm. Eleven ministers would also participate in the ceremony, including Reverend William George McCloskey, Bishop of Louisville and Reverend Camilius Paul Maes, Bishop of Covington.[ccxlv]

On February 12, 1909, hundreds of attendees watched in the cold drizzle as President Roosevelt laid the cornerstone for the Lincoln Memorial. After the celebration, a centenary service was to be held at Temple Adath Israel. Governor Willison and hundreds of people attended the service. Judge W.C. Harris and Col. Andrew Cowan gave speeches on Lincoln. Harris was to give his view of Lincoln as a Southerner and Cowan was to give his view of Lincoln as a Northerner.[ccxlvi]

In his speech, Cowan stated that he directed the cannons at the Battle of Sailor's Creek against the Confederates. At the battle, the last gun of the artillery brigade of the Sixth Corps, which Cowan commanded was fired. The first opposed to the Federal artillery was Confederate General Richard Ewell's Corps of General Robert E. Lee's army. They were surrounded by Union General Armstrong Custer's cavalry and the Sixth Corps of Infantry and Artillery and that night, just as darkness fell, Cowan saw eleven thousand Confederate soldiers surrender to the Union forces.

He stated in the speech that Kentucky was famous for beautiful, gracious, queenly women who bred men. "Their sires blaze the forest trail and made the Wilderness Road. They paddled their canoes and steered their boats down the tawny waters of the Ohio from its source to the mouth. God showed them their land of Canaan and they went down and took it from the heathen. In this beautiful land of forest and stream, of hill and dale, of the bluegrass and the beargrass, they and their descendant's made the 'Old Kentucky Home'. Statesmen, jurist, scholars, preachers, hunters, soldiers and merchants-their names and deeds are woven into the history of the State and of the Nation."[ccxlvii]

Cowan stated that when war divided the states into North and South and into armed camps, Jefferson Davis, a Kentuckian born into affluence, already famous in the South, commanded the Confederacy, and Abraham Lincoln, born in Kentucky in a cabin, was a self-made man and self-educated, "the untried choice of an untried political party, held the old ship of state true to her course through four years of bloody war, bringing her into the haven of peace at last with the old flag flying, bloody and torn, but with not a star missing from its azure field."[ccxlviii]

Cowan finished his speech by stating that he stood "today at the little log cabin wherein he was born, down on that poor farm in Kentucky, feeling that surely God raised up this wonderful man for the saving of the Nation and the emancipation of a race. Our God, in whom we trust, will still use the people of this great nation for His omnipotent purposes, and can raise the humblest to do his will. God has sounded forth the trumpet, which has never known defeat; He is searching out the hearts of men before his judgment-seat; Oh, be swift, our souls to answer Him, be jubilant, our feet; Our God is marching on."[ccxlix] After Cowan's speech, Professor Albion Small gave his speech "Abraham Lincoln, the Prophet of Democracy," followed by Dr. Ignatius Mueller.

Two years later, the Lincoln memorial building was complete and a similar dedication took place. President William Howard Taft dedicated the new memorial building. The building was designed by John Russell Pope and was in the majestic Beaux Arts style and housed the log cabin birthplace. The Lincoln Farm Association also undertook a serious investigation of the cabin's authenticity, and was satisfied that the cabin was Lincoln's birthplace. Recent research and carbon dating have proved that the cabin is not Lincoln's original cabin. The cabin inside the memorial dates to the 19th Century, but is not the original. The fifty-six steps ascend to the building representing each year that Lincoln was alive and the sixteen panels above the ceiling represent Lincoln as the 16th President. Above the memorial building is inscribed, "Here over the log cabin where Abraham Lincoln was born, destined to preserve the Union and free the slave, a grateful people have dedicated this memorial to unity, peace, and brotherhood among the states." In 1916, the Lincoln Memorial was given over to Federal authorities, and the National Park Service assumed ownership and management of the site.

Chapter 18

The 50th Anniversary of the Battle of Gettysburg

On September 19, 1911, in Providence, Rhode Island, Cowan was elected Grand Commander of the Army of the Potomac Society and General. The following year, the country prepared for the 50th Anniversary of the Battle of Gettysburg. Louisville would be represented at the celebration by four officers who took part in the battle. Lieutenant General Walker, commander in chief of the United Confederate Veterans called for those who wore the gray to join the Union veterans in making the event a peace memorial to mark the healing of all the scars of the Civil War. Only three Confederates and one Union soldier who participated in the battle remained alive. General Walker called attention to the recent act of Congress for providing for the erection of a peace memorial on the battlefield, and the state of Pennsylvania giving $250,000 to help pay for the expense of holding the celebration. Every state in the Union and the territories were called upon to name a commissioner to the celebration and give money to pay the traveling expenses of all the survivors of the Battle of Gettysburg. Colonel Cowan was Louisville's only remaining survivor of the battle and was appointed commissioner for Kentucky.[ccl]

Cowan stated that since very few Kentuckians took part in the battle on either side, state legislators would not raise money to defray the traveling costs for the survivors to Gettysburg. The four remaining survivors had to pay their own way. The Confederate survivors of the Battle of Gettysburg were Major John Leathers, who was in Confederate General Stonewall Jackson's Brigade, Captain George Norton, who was on E.P. Alexander's staff, and Major Abner Harris, who was attached to Confederate General Fitzhugh Lee's staff.

On May 29, 1912, two Kentuckians attended the meeting of the Battle of Gettysburg Commission. They were Rear Admiral John Watson, United States Navy, and Colonel Andrew Cowan. Watson, Cowan and the other commissioners went to go see Congress in support of bills, pending in the House and Senate, providing an appropriation for $150,000 for the Gettysburg 50th Anniversary celebration planned for July 1 through July 5, 1913. The commission hoped that 40,000 veterans would attend the event. In order to care for veterans, the town of Gettysburg would have to be reconstructed, including the surrounding area.[ccli]

On July 1 through July 5, 1913, over fifty thousand veterans attended the Gettysburg reunion. The highlight of the reunion was the laying of a cornerstone for the peace memorial on the battlefield, but the plans for the memorial fell through. Cowan revived the plan and during a meeting he attended he recommended sending a committee went to Washington with the intent of introducing a bill to Congress, which would provide for the erection of a peace monument and the appropriation of one million dollars. In addressing the crowd at Gettysburg, Cowan stated that…

> *"It is hard to control my emotions when I recall this battlefield fifty years ago. Pickett's brave men were in full retreat and we were holding the ground in the Angle. Beyond the Emmittsburg Road was thickly strewn with their dead and wounded and our own.*[cclii]
>
> *Over there on Cemetery Ridge stands today an equestrian statue of General George Meade, the great commander of the Army of the Potomac, facing Seminary Ridge. Does he look for the peerless leader of the Southern army?*[ccliii]
>
> *Gen. Robert E. Lee's lifelike statue, mounted on his famous war horse Traveller, soon will be placed on the pedestal already raised by Virginia on Seminary Ridge to receive it. The forms of the two great commanders on the battlefield of Gettysburg will be there to stand facing each other while time endures. Behind us a little way, at the clump of trees, is a monument which marks the high tide of the war on this field. This grand celebration of the fiftieth anniversary of the battle of Gettysburg marks a high tide of peace between the North and South which shall never recede while Americans love liberty and the Union, and the cornerstone of a monument has been laid on Put-in-Bay Island in commemorations of the centennial of Perry's victory over the British fleet on Lake Erie.*[ccliv]
>
> *Such monuments possess an educational value which cannot be measured by what they cost. Teach the young Americans to believe that we can have no fears for the future of our country.*[cclv]

Should not a peace monument be raised on this battlefield at Gettysburg, a monument in commemoration of this Union between the soldiers who fought for different principles bravely from 1861 to 1865 by and through which has been forever established that this nation under God shall not perish?[cclvi]

We should highly resolve to do all that in us lies to influence the Congress and the States to erect a peace monument which shall be higher and grander than any other now here or hereafter to be erected on the battlefield of Gettysburg.[cclvii]

After the Gettysburg reunion, a committee of veterans visited Washington, D.C. with the hopes of obtaining financial support from Congress. Congress informed the veterans that there was no hope for a congressional bill to appropriate funding for the monument until the next fiscal budget. Cowan did not give up on his dream of a peace memorial.[cclvii]

Cowan continued to push for a Peace Memorial at Gettysburg. On September 19, 1913, Cowan traveled to Chattanooga, Tennessee to launch the Gettysburg Peace Memorial Association. The Association comprised of thirty-four Confederate veterans, including Louisville residents General W.B. Haldeman, Major John Leathers, and George Norton and thirty-four Federal veterans, including Louisville residents Andrew Cowan and Captain Americus Whedon. Cowan was a board of directors member of the Association.[cclix]

The purpose of the Association was to obtain from the United States Congress appropriations together with appointment of a commission to erect a peace monument on the battlefield at Gettysburg in commemoration of the fiftieth anniversary of the battle on July 1 through 4, 1913, between more than fifty thousand veterans of the Civil War, both North and South. The meeting between the Confederate and Union veterans in peace, good will and loyalty, marked the harmonious unification of the nation as one people with a common destiny and should be commemorated with a peace monument on the battlefield, which would serve to exalt the sentiment and responsibility of national patriotism with all the people of the United States.[cclx]

On October 4, 1913, Cowan was re-elected president of the Army of the Potomac veterans association and Confederate Major John Leathers was made an honorary member of the Army of the Potomac veteran's organization. The Army of the Potomac organization voted to indorse Cowan's Gettysburg Memorial Association.[cclxi]

Although Cowan devoted the rest of his life to the erection of a Peace Memorial at Gettysburg, he would not live to see his dream fulfilled. The Eternal Light Peace Memorial would have to wait until the seventy-fifth reunion of the Battle of Gettysburg. On July 3, 1938, President Franklin D. Roosevelt addressed the public before he unveiled the peace memorial with the eternal flame. To help pay for the memorial, in 1936, Congress authorized the raising of funding for the monument by issuing fifty thousand half dollar commemorative coins. President Roosevelt also allocated nine hundred thousand dollars for the transportation and camp accommodations for the twenty-five veterans who fought at Gettysburg, along with 1,359 Union veterans and 486 Confederate veterans.

On May 7, 1914, Cowan was elected commander of the Ohio Branch of the Military Commandery of the Loyal Legion in Cincinnati, Ohio. The Loyal Legion was founded at Philadelphia on April 15, 1865, after the death of President Lincoln. The Legion was a patriotic order, comprised of commissioned officers of the United States army and navy, like the Order of Cincinnati. During the Loyal Legion banquet, Former President William Taft was speaker at the assembly of the Loyal Legion.[cclxii] During the banquet, Cowan gave a speech. In his speech, he stated the April 9, 1914 Tampico affair, which led to the Battle of Veracruz and the United States occupation of Veracruz during the Mexican revolution. In his speech, he stated that he…

"had been born in time to be a comrade of yours through the four years of dreadful war, waged to preserve the Union. We have lived to see its results accepted by men of the South who fought so valiantly for disunion and the Confederacy. We have become united forever in allegiance to one flag, the glorious flag of a mighty nation. The land of the free and the home of the brave. Our country, right or wrong, commands our devotion, our fortunes and our lives. Many thousands of our brave boys are on the firing line tonight in Mexico, and our old hearts are with them. Today and again tonight I have heard the condition down there described as an imbroglio. I call it War! Nearly a hundred of our sons have already fallen there, dead or wounded. When the sword is drawn, like that I call it War, describe it how they may. I am glad that General (Frederick) Funston, in command at Vera Cruz, had today been given authority to advance his troops as far as he deems necessary."[cclxiii]

During the speech, Cowan drew the sword that was on the banquet table. He then exclaimed:

> *"Forward to the highlands on the road to Mexico City! Away from Vera Cruz, a pesthole in the tropical summer! Plague and pestilence may there claim the lives of hundreds of our un-acclimated soldiers. Disease is far more to be feared for them than shot and shell. Remember Scott's army waiting long for supplies and reinforcements on that same road to Mexico City, not on the deadly tropical coast, but in wholesome altitudes fifty miles or more inland, where his little army waited in safety from the danger of tropical plague. Forward General Funston. If you be worthy of the great soldiers of your State, Grant, Sherman and Sheridan and of Scott, the greatest soldier of his time, you should deem it necessary to advance your men to those same hills near Jalapa before the enemy fortifies them against you. The A.B.C. powers may then medicate Canada all summer long, and we will be patient if our sons are safe from the danger of pestilence. And we will pray that peace with honor may come through mediation, however prolonged.... War is no picnic, as we who enlisted in the earliest enthusiasm of the first call for volunteers in April 1861 soon found out. It means hard and exhaustive work, coarse toll often for the men in the ranks, exposure to disease with consequent loss of healthy or life, long, and perhaps, before they may taste the excitements of campaigns and battles. The hardest services that volunteer soldiers must endure brings no glory like that won in the storms of battle, yet no soldier can escape the hardest service if he does his duty.... Our young men will be better soldiers if they go forth-as they must go when their country calls-knowing the serious nature of the service before them. They will be prepared to stand by the colors, even in the face of certain death. The blood of our sons is precious, but the nation's honor is worth more than life."*

During the banquet, Union General J. Warren Keifer mentioned Cowan's service career in the Sixth Army Corps during the Civil War. Keifer commanded the Third Division, in the Sixth Corps. Cowan responded to Keifer, stating that he was one of the ablest and bravest of the commanders who wore the Union uniform. The crowd broke out in applause. Cowan mentioned in his speech that Keifer held Cowan's receipt for eight cannons that his division captured in the assault on the Confederate works at Petersburg on April 2, 1865. Cowan stated he remembered twenty-three cannons captured that morning and he sent all of them back behind the Union breastworks and forts. General Keifer was the only division commander who required the chief of artillery of the corps to give a written receipt for his trophies.

Cowan closed his speech stating that the bonds of comradeship and friendship and the ties of patriotism bound the members of the Loyal Legion together and that he was thankful for having served in the Union army, who fought and bled so that the Nation might live. He quoted: "There are bonds of all sorts in this world of ours, Fetters of friendship and ties of flowers, And true lovers' knots, I ween. The boys and the girls are bound by a kiss, But there's never a bond, old friend, like this: We have drunk from the same canteen!" The crowd broke out in applause and the Glee Club sang the song "We've Drunk from the Same Canteen," which ended the banquet.[cclxiv]

Chapter 19

The Confederate Veterans Reunion: 1917

On July 3, 1915, at a meeting of the Second Corps Society in Washington, Cowan proposed that the United Confederate Veterans be invited to hold their annual encampment in 1917 in the nation's capital. He felt that to crown the everlasting establishment of unity between the Union and Confederate soldiers, which took place at Gettysburg two years before, he felt that the Confederate veterans should be able to hold their convention in Washington, D.C. When he asked if the Second Corps society would entertain the idea, there was silence in the room for a moment while the full meaning of the proposed invitation was sinking in, then the realization of the significance of a Confederate encampment in Washington dawned, the soldiers of the Second Corps rose and cheered, giving Cowan his endorsement of the invitation.[cclxv]

Colonel Hilary A. Herbert of the 8th Alabama Infantry, ex-Secretary of the Navy, and a lawyer in Washington, accepted the invitation for the Confederate Veterans, to whom he was commissioned to carry the invitation. General Nelson A. Miles endorsed the invitation. Cowan was asked while staying at the Waldorf-Astoria how he came up with the idea of a reunion of Confederate Veterans in Washington. He stated that almost fifty years ago he went to Kentucky to live. A Yankee in one of the hotbeds of secession, he at first was scarcely welcome. The hatred and bitterness of the war were still too fresh in the memory of the defeated Southerners. But Cowan stayed in Louisville, he made friends with the men against whom he fought and gradually he saw the hostility of Southerners receding in their hearts before patriotism for the United States.

Three years prior, Cowan was made an honorary member of the Orphan Brigade of Kentucky Confederates and two years previously, he met the Confederate Veterans at Gettysburg. During that time, with others, he laid the plans for the erection by Congress of a monument on the battlefield at Gettysburg to commemorate the reunion and Cowan was still devoting much of his time to the fruition of his monument. Cowan conceived of the idea of the Confederate reunion in Washington when he was on the reviewing stand in Washington several days prior, that he noticed three Confederate soldiers in gray marching with a Massachusetts post, each supporting on either side by a comrade in blue, and Cowan was glad. Cowan saw those comrades in blue and gray marching arm in arm, that he thought that a reunion in Washington would be patriotic and inspiring and the capstone of peace and good will.[cclxvi]

On November 11, 1915, Cowan was congratulated for his suggestion at the reunion of the Grand Army of the Republic that the United Confederate Veterans be invited to hold their 1917 convention in Washington, D.C. Eli Torrance, former commander of the G.A.R., wrote to Cowan approving of the suggestion and hoped that the Confederates would accept the invitation. He stated that for years he favored action on the part of the government to supplement the aid extending to the inhabitants of the Confederate Veterans homes by public taxation in the South. He supported the American soldier in receiving food, shelter and raiment without discrimination and independent of the color of the uniform they wore. He wrote to Cowan that the significance of supporting the Confederate homes by the government would suggest that the war was over, that the Confederate soldiers are now true citizens of the republic, and that the Confederate soldier should be recognized for his courage and heroism, which are the nation's most valuable asset. The support of Confederate homes would be a token of the nation's admiration, respect, and affection and help heal old wounds and remove any bitterness.

General George Pickett's wife also wrote to Cowan, endorsing his suggestion of the Confederate reunion in Washington, D.C. She wrote to Cowan that his "whole life has been given to peace and reunion and loyalty to all that is best in the ideals of our republic, and no partisan narrowness ever mars your work for the good and the true."[cclxvii]

On October 12, 1915, at Gettysburg, a statue of Union General Alexander Webb was unveiled at the "Bloody Angle" where General Webb and his men of the Philadelphia Brigade met the divisions of Confederate Generals George Pickett and J. Johnston Pettigrew as they mounted the wall in their last desperate effort to penetrate the Union line on the third day at Gettysburg. Fifty Union veterans who withstood the onslaught were present during the unveiling to honor their commander. When the American flag that was covering Webb's statue was removed, the Third United States Field Artillery fired thirteen cannons. A granddaughter of General Webb, Miss Anne R. Alexander pulled the cord. After the dedicatory services, a procession was held through the streets of Gettysburg. At the monument, New York Governor Whitman delivered a eulogy of General Webb. Colonel Cowan also made a speech. General Horatio King delivered his poem "Gettysburg."[cclxviii]

On the fiftieth anniversary of Lincoln's death, Cowan addressed a letter to the Mayor John Buschemeyer of Louisville expressing his pride in the mayor's proclamation directing that all public buildings would have their flags at half-mast and urging all citizens to observe the day. Cowan hoped that Lincoln would be revered as much as Washington. Cowan wrote to the mayor that he saw the war end with the Army of Northern Virginia surrender at Appomattox. He saw the President at Washington, in camp and on the battle front, under fire, and he even felt Lincoln's hand shake.[cclxix]

He stated that he lived to see hatred and bitterness engendered by the war and politics obliterated and the growth of mutual respect between the survivors of the "blue and gray" in Louisville and throughout the country.[cclxx]

Cowan stated that the birthplace in Hodgenville, Kentucky was marked with a memorial building which enshrined the rebuilt log cabin. At the rotunda of the new Kentucky state capitol at Frankfort was a bronze statue of Lincoln, a gift from the state by James Breckinridge Speed. Cowan mentioned that the Lincoln Farm Memorial Association was ready to transfer the Lincoln farm to the State of Kentucky, along with a large amount of money for the monument's preservation.[cclxxi]

Cowan thought that the farm should be developed and maintained as a nursery for every tree and shrub indigenous to the soil. The sale of the trees and shrubs would repay for the cost within a few years. He asked all Kentuckians to unite and demand that the next Kentucky legislature receive the gift of the Lincoln Farm Association. The Military Order of the Loyal Legion observed the fiftieth anniversary of Lincoln's death on April 14, 15 and 16 in Philadelphia. Cowan planned to attend the event even though he was on crutches and dependent on help. His illness was caused by a gunshot wound he received in the Civil War.[cclxxii]

In closing his letter to the mayor, he stated that although he was not a native of Kentucky, and not a native born American, his children and grandchildren were born in Kentucky. He loved to tell the story of what he had seen in Kentucky through the fifty years that he had lived in Louisville. He watched as the city grew into a more tolerant and united people, and that the soldiers of the South and soldiers of the North "with malice towards none and charity toward all" were equally loyal to the flag that stood for an emblem of a united nation.[cclxxiii]

The Confederate Veterans accepted Cowan's invitation to host their reunion in Washington, D.C. Thousands of veterans and visitors attended the reunion of the United Confederate Veterans reunion. The attendees gave President Woodrow Wilson a great ovation when he welcome the ex-Confederate soldiers to the capital and told them that the country was beginning to understand that one of the purposes of Providence in keeping the nation united was to meet the opportunity now before America to fight for liberty and mankind.[cclxxiv]

President Wilson declared that the day was one of gladness because of the memories and of a rededication of a united country to those principles that had made America great among the nations. While waiting for the President, the crowd cheered for the Confederate leaders, and the U.S. Marine band playing and gray jacked women from Portsmouth singing Confederate songs.[cclxxv]

When the President mounted the platform, the Confederate veterans waved their hats and the hall echoed with the Rebel yell. Many of the veterans shook the President's hand. The keynote of the opening session of the reunion was patriotism. The presentation of the United States flag to General George P. Harrison, commander in chief of the Confederates by Colonel Andrew Cowan of the Grand Army of the Republic, was the signal for a demonstration. The Stars and Stripes hung side by side with the Stars and Bars behind the presiding officer and remained throughout the reunion.[cclxxvi]

Chapter 20

The Death of Colonel Andrew Cowan

On August 23, 1919, Colonel Cowan died at his home at the age of seventy-eight. During his lifetime, he sailed to American from Ayshire, Scotland to America. At a young age, he joined the Union army and enlisted in a New York regiment and later the 1st New York Independent Battery. He fought at several Eastern Theater battles during the Civil War, including the Seven Days Campaign, with the battles of Williamsburg, Antietam, Fredericksburg, Chancellorsville, the James River and Rappahannock Campaign, Spottsylvania Courthouse, Bloody Angle, Cold Harbor, Petersburg, Weldon Railroad, repulse of Early's attack on Washington, D.C., Gilbert's Ford, where he was wounded on September 13, returned to duty on October 23, and appointed chief of artillery of the 6th Corps on December 21, 1864, siege and fall of Petersburg, Sailor's Creek, and the surrender at Appomattox. He was especially known for his actions at Gettysburg during Pickett's charge defending the "Bloody Angle." After the War, he was widely known as the father of the joint reunion of the Blue and Gray at Gettysburg on the fiftieth anniversary of the Battle of Gettysburg. He headed the firm of Andrew Cowan & Company, established in 1866, as a wholesale hardware, leather, and mill supplies in Louisville. He was president of the National Oak Leather Company, director of the National Bank of Commerce, Fidelity, and Columbia Trust Company. He was a member of the first and second Boards of the Park Commissioners, which established the Louisville Park System in 1891-1895, and was president of the board in 1907-1908. He was a trustee of the American Printing House of the Blind, from 1897 to until his death and president of the Kentucky Institute for the Education of the Blind from 1898 to 1900 and 1908 to 1918, and also a former president of the Society of the Army of the Potomac.[cclxxvii]

He was also a member of the Pendennis Club, Salmagundi Club, the Filson Historical Society, the Conservation Club, and the Army Corps.

He took an active part in Manual Training High School and was elected to the school board. Cowan was also a leader in the effort to secure a new site for a new Male High (Classical) School building and was one of the largest contributors to the fund. He was an organizer and charter member of the Council of the Charity Organization Society. He was a trustee of the Louisville Free Kindergarten Association. He was also a life member of the American Civil Association. Cowan was a Republican and in 1908 he was a delegate to the National Republican Convention. He was also a Baptist. He was in military organizations, such as the member of the Grand Army of the Republic, president of the Society of the Army of the Potomac, 1911 to 1916, commander of the Ohio Chapter of the Military Order of the Loyal Legion from 1914 to 1916, and junior vice commander in chief of the same order from 1915 to 1918. The Kentucky Orphan Brigade members made him an honorary member, despite Cowan being in the Union Army. Cowan was one of the most staunchest friends of the Confederate Home in Pee Wee Valley, Oldham County, Kentucky and donated gifts and took a personal interest in the welfare of the home.

He was survived by his widow, Anna Gilbert Cowan and his son, Gilbert Cowan. He had four grandchildren, Gilbert Cowan, Jr., Embry S. Cowan, Mary B. Cowan, and Marjorie Cowan and two great granddaughters-in-law, Margaret Cowan and Mrs. Embry Cowan.

When his death reached the news of city leaders, the flag on city hall was lowered at half-mast. When Henry Watterson learned of Cowan's death, he issued a statement:

> "*Col. Andrew Cowan has been for half a century one of the leading citizens of Louisville. He came to Kentucky just after the War of Sections and engaged at once actively in the business life and public affairs of the city. He had a splendid record as an artillery officer on the Union side of the great sectional controversy, gaining great celebrity with Cowan's battery at Gettysburg, the real hero of the bloody angle. To me he was a life-long friend, and, though prepared for it, I am deeply distressed by his going.*"[cclxxviii]

Former Governor of Kentucky Augustus E. Willson wrote a tribute to Cowan. He stated that Cowan was…

"*one of the best and most useful of men, the highest type of citizen, a soldier and a gentleman through and through.... As a citizen, he has always been one of the most sensible, useful and valuable men in Kentucky and has thought, studied, worked and fought for the highest ideals of life, Government and liberty and has waged unceasing war against every public wrong or abuse and for every useful reform that has been brought to pass in this city and State for half a century.*[cclxxix]

He was one of the first in the struggle for the establishment to free Louisville from hurtful local political conditions kept up in the interest of our utility corporations. In the noble fight over the new charter of the gas company, he was a leader and a power which achieved results for the god of the people.

In the crisis of the contested election of Governor Taylor and the grave troubles at Frankfort, he was one of the bravest and best of all who strove to uphold the law and order, visiting Frankfort frequently and present in every council held to preserve order, defend the right and secure justice.

In every important public emergency, in every great reform, in every noble charity, in every public spirited undertaking, he was one of the first to suggest and plan for the public welfare and always one of the first and most generous to give money as well as work and thought.

His soul was a stranger to compromise or expediency with wrong, unfairness or in any matter of principle. His courage and firmness as a soldier were renewed in firm and determined attitude as a citizen and even as a friend.

He was a dutiful son and brother, a noble and true and devoted husband and father, and he will be long remembered with love, affection and admiration. The most valuable trait and best remembered characteristic of Col. Cowan was his unshakable will to be just and he kept the faith until his death.

On August 24, 1919, Cowan had a brief and simple funeral service in his residence, Alloway House, Ayrstead. The body was covered with a United States flag and lowered into the grave at Cave Hill Cemetery as a soldier from Camp Zachary Taylor played Taps. The Revered Dr. W. W. Landrum, pastor of the Broadway Baptist Church, conducted the services assisted by Reverend Charles E. Cralk, dean emeritus of the Christ Church Cathedral and the Reverend Dr. Peyton H. Hoge, pastor of the Pee Wee Valley Presbyterian Church, as requested by Colonel Cowan.[cclxxx]

Five of the eleven members of the Army Post found in Louisville by Captain Alfred Pirtle, of which Cowan had been president, attended the funeral. The members were Captain Pirtle, W.O. Bonnie, Colonel John Gathright, Albert Scott, and B.F.D. Fitch. Mayor George Weissinger Smith and Mrs. Smith, members of the Board of Park Commissioners, Major John H. Leathers, Alexander Barrett and many others of prominence in the city attended the funeral. The flag on city hall and all municipal buildings in Louisville were at half-mast.

When the will was read after Cowan's funeral, the bulk of his estate was to be held in trust for the benefit of his widow Anna Gilbert Cowan. Cowan's estate amounted to $350,000 of personal value and $100,000 in property. If you factor in the value of inflation, Cowan's estate was worth $6,188,150.00 today. Three employees of Cowan & Company, Florian Crush, secretary treasurer, J.W.G. Hughes, assistant manager, and Louis Mattingly, chief bookkeeper, were also remembered in the will. Crush and Hughes each purchased $3,000 of the common stock and Mr. Mattingly purchased $1,000 worth of stock, each giving his amount to Cowan. In his will, Cowan instructed the executor and trustee to cancel the notes and return them to the makers and in addition repay to them any part of the principal that had been paid and all interest at the rate of 4 percent for all such payments from the date of the payments until cancellation of the notes.[cclxxxi]

Cowan stated that at the time the notes were executed it was expected that dividends from the common stock would enable them to pay the notes in three years, and that the gift to them was in recognition of their faithful service and unwavering loyalty to the firm, with which they had been associated in responsible positions since early boyhood.

Gilbert Cowan received two hundred shares of the capital stock of the firm, and Gilbert Cowan, Jr. and May Embry Swearingen Cowan, grandson and granddaughter, each received $1,000 dollars in Liberty bonds, which was equivalent to $13,000 dollars today. Mrs. Mary Embry Curd Cowan, daughter-in-law, received twenty shares of stock of the First National Bank and twenty shares of the capital stock the Kentucky Title Savings Bank & Trust Company, to be held in trust for her for life, at her death the income was to be paid to her children for a period of ten years, when the children would receive the principal.

Margaret Cowan, widow of Albert Cowan, deceased son of Colonel Cowan, received 200 shares of preferred stock of Andrew Cowan & Company to be held in trust for her for life, and Mary and Marjorie

Cowan, children of Albert Cowan, each received 200 shares of the preferred and fifty shares of the common stock of the firm to be held in trust for them for life. George Cowan, an invalid brother living in San Francisco, was paid $50.00 a month for life, and each employee of the firm of Andrew Cowan & Company was to receive $50.00 for five years and each servant received $100.00 in cash or $1,375 today.

The remainder of the estate was to be held in trust for his widow and she was to receive the income semi-annually and after her death one half of the income was to be paid to Gilbert S. Cowan and one fourth to Marjorie and Mary Cowan, grandchildren.

After Cowan's death, the Board of Park Commissioners began a movement to erect a memorial for Andrew Cowan. The memorial to Cowan would be placed in Cherokee Park, near where he lived for many years prior to his death. The committee proposed that a large bronze tablet would be erected and the tablet would list the accomplishments that Cowan took in erecting and building Louisville's park system. The park commissioners mentioned that John B. Castleman already had an equestrian statue at the entrance of Cherokee park and Cowan along with Charles Jacob should have a monument.[cclxxxii]

By 1921, the Andrew Cowan & Company expanded their business scope. Gilbert Cowan added a line of shoe findings, saddlery, hardware and mill supplies. When the automobile arrived in Louisville, the company was the first to add a complete line of auto supplies and accessories and outgrew their business at 423 West Main Street, and moved their tire and battery service department to 523 East Broadway. The business name changed to Acco Service. Cowan & Company on 423 West Main Street continued to carry a large stock of mill supplies, transmission machinery, harnesses, and saddle leather, hardware and auto accessories, as well as a leather belt company. Gilbert Cowan continued to run the business.[cclxxxiii]

CONCLUSION

During his lifetime, Cowan lived the American dream. When his family left Scotland for a better life, they hoped their son would be able to achieve the American dream. Cowan received an education, fought bravely for his newly adopted country during the Civil War in some of the most horrific battles, such as Antietam and Gettysburg, became a successive businessman, and amassed a fortune in his business of Andrew Cowan & Company. He felt so proud to being an American and Louisville inhabitant that he gave back to his country and his community. He helped found the Louisville Parks System and gave to schools, such as the American School for the Blind, Manual High School and other educational institutions.

The Civil War deeply affected him and he devoted his life to peace and the mending of wounds between the Union and Confederate veterans. He was the founder of the Blue and Gray reunion at Gettysburg reunion in 1887 and in 1895 during the Grand Army of the Republic Reunion in Louisville, Kentucky, he wanted the theme of the reunion to be one of reconciliation and peace. In 1905, during the Confederate Reunion in Louisville, the Confederate veterans honored Cowan for his efforts for the care and welfare of his former combatants and made him the only honorary member of the Kentucky Orphan Brigade. Cowan was one of the most staunchest friends of the Confederate Home in Pee Wee Valley, Oldham County, Kentucky, and donated gifts and took a personal interest in the welfare of the home. At the fiftieth anniversary of the Battle of Gettysburg Reunion, Cowan advocated a peace memorial at Gettysburg. Cowan also invited the Confederate Veterans to have their reunion in 1917 at Washington, D.C.

He wanted to make sure that Americans would never fight against Americans again. Contemporaries and present historians may view Cowan as the hero of Gettysburg at the "Bloody Angle," but with this book, hopefully history may see Cowan as much more. Hopefully he will be seen as a contributor to Louisville's history with what we now know as the Metro Park System and a peacemaker.

Endnotes

[i] Cowan Funeral Set For Today, *The Louisville Courier-Journal*, August 24, 1919; Col. Andrew Cowan Dead, Father of the Joint Reunion of Blue and Gray at Gettysburg, *The New York Times*, August 24, 1919.

[ii] Glorify Name of Lincoln: All Elements Unite in Service to His Memory, *The Louisville Courier-Journal*, Feb. 13, 1909.

[iii] *A History of Kentucky and Kentuckians: The Leaders, Representative Men in Commerce, Industry, and Modern Activities*, Volume II, Lewis Publishing Company, Chicago & New York, 1912, 1024-1026.

[iv] Ibid.

[v] R.L. Murray, *Hurrah for the Ould Flag: Captain Andrew Cowan and the First New York Independent Battery at Gettysburg*, Benedum Books, New York, 1998, 4-5.

[vi] The "Bloody Angle:" Thrilling Story of the Crisis of the Battle of Gettysburg, *Louisville Courier-Journal*, July 9, 1911.

[vii] Murray, *Hurrah of the Ould Flag*, 6.

[viii] Ibid, 6.

[ix] Ibid, 7.

[x] Patricia Faust, Editor, *Historical Times Illustrated Encyclopedia of the Civil War,* (Harper & Row, New York, 1986), 755; Ronald Baley, *Forward to Richmond: McClellan's Peninsular Campaign*, 89.

[xi] Murray, *Hurrah for the Ould Flag, 10.*

[xii] Murray, *Hurrah for the Ould Flag*, 12.

[xiii] Patricia Faust, *Historical Times Illustrated Encyclopedia of the Civil War*, 571.

[xiv] Ronald Bailey, *Forward to Richmond: McClellan's Peninsular Campaign*, 93.

[xv] Patricia Faust, editor, *Historical Times Illustrated Encyclopedia of the Civil War*, 32; Stewart Sifakis, *Who Was Who In the Union*, Vol. I, 14-15.

[xvi] Bailey, *Forward to Richmond*, 94.

[xvii] R.L. Murray, *Hurrah for the Ould Flag*," Benedeum Books, 21.

[xviii] Bailey, 106-107.

[xix] O.R. Series I, Vol. XI/1 May 5, 1862, Battle of Williamsburg, No 49, Report of General Winfield S. Hancock, U.S. Army, Commanding First Brigade.

[xx] O.R. Series I, Vol. XI/1 May 5, 1862, Battle of Williamsburg, No 49, Report of General Winfield S. Hancock, U.S. Army, Commanding First Brigade.

[xxi] Ibid.

[xxii] O.R. Series I, Vol. XI/1 May 5, 1862. Battle of Williamsburg, Va., Report Number 48. Reports of Lieutenant Andrew Cowan, First New York Battery.

[xxiii] O.R. Series I, Vol. XI/1 May 5, 1862. Battle of Williamsburg, Va., Report Number 48. Reports of Lieutenant Andrew Cowan, First New York Battery.

[xxiv] O.R. Series I, Vol. XI/1 May 5, 1862, Battle of Williamsburg, No 49, Report of General Winfield S. Hancock, U.S. Army, Commanding First Brigade.

[xxv] O.R. Series I, Vol. XI/1, May 8, 1862, Battle of Williamsburg, Lieutenant Andrew Cowan, Commanding First New York Battery, Capt. C. C. Wheeler, Commanding Battery E, First New York Artillery.

[xxvi] Ibid.

[xxvii] O.R. Series I, Vol. XI/1, May 5, 1862, Battle of Williamsburg, No. 49, Report for General Winfield S. Hancock, U. S. Army, Commanding the First Brigade.

[xxviii] Ibid.

[xxix] William Davis, *The Battlefields of the Civil War*, Salamander Books, New York, 59.

[xxx] Patricia Faust, *Historical Times Illustrated Encyclopedia of the Civil War*, 19.

[xxxi] Glorify the Name of Lincoln: All Elements Unite in Service to His Memory, *The Louisville Courier-Journal*, Feb. 13, 1909.

[xxxii] Ibid.

[xxxiii] Ibid.

[xxxiv] Ibid.

[xxxv] Patricia Faust, *Historical Times Illustrated Encyclopedia of the Civil War*, 19-20.

[xxxvi] Patricia Faust, editor, *Historical Times Illustrated Encyclopedia of the Civil War*, 20.

[xxxvii] Ibid, 20.

[xxxviii] Ibid.

[xxxix] Robert Bailey, *The Bloodiest Day: The Battle of Antietam*, (Time Life Book, Alexandria, Virginia, 1984), 66-83; Patricia Faust, *Historical Times Illustrated Encyclopedia of the Civil War*, 19.

[xl] Stephen Foster, *The Battle of Antietam*, Civil War Cards, Atlas Editions.

[xli] Robert Bailey, *The Bloodiest Day: The Battle of Antietam*, (Time Life Book, Alexandria, Virginia, 1984), 86-95.

[xlii] Ibid, 93-99; Stephen Foster, *The Civil War Cards: The People, The Places, The Politics, The Action; The Battle of Sharpsburg*, (Atlas Editions, Durham, Connecticut), 1994.

[xliii] Stephen Foster, *The Civil War Cards: The People, The Places, The Politics, The Action: The Battle of Sharpsburg*, (Atlas Editions, Durham, Connecticut), 1994.

[xliv] Robert Bailey, *The Bloodiest Day: The Battle of Antietam*, (Time Life Book, Alexandria, Virginia, 1984), 120-129; Stephen Foster, *Civil War Cards: Battle of Sharpsburg*, Atlas Editions, 1994.

[xlv] Joseph Pierro, editor, *The Maryland Campaign of September of 1862; Ezra A. Carman's Definitive Study of the Union and Confederate Armies at Antietam*, (Routledge, New York, 2008), 299-301.

[xlvi] R.L. Murray, "Hurrah for the Ould Flag!," Captain Andrew Cowan and the First New York Independent Battery at Gettsyburg, Benedum Books, 1998, 40.

[xlvii] O.R. Series I, Vol. XIX/1 Sept 3-20, The Maryland Campaign. No. 128, Report of Capt. Andrew Cowan, commanding First New York Battery, of the Battle of Antietam.

[xlviii] Ibid, 45.

[xlix] Patricia Faust, editor, *Historical Times Illustrated Encyclopedia of the Civil War*, 288-289; Stephen T. Foster, *The Civil War Cards: The People, The Places, The Politics, The Action: Battle of Fredericksburg*, (Atlas Editions, Durham, Connecticut), 1994.

[l] Stewart Sifakis, *Who Was Who in the Union*, Vol. I, Facts of File, Inc., New York, 1988, 205-206.

[li] O.R. Series I, Vol. XXI, Battle of Fredericksburg, No. 22. Reports of Brig. Gen. Henry J. Hunt, U. S. Army, Chief of Artillery.

[lii] O.R. Series I, Vol. XXI, No. 47. Report of Capt Gustavus De Russy, 4th U.S. Artillery, commanding batteries on the left; *O.R.* Series I, Vol. XXI, Dec. 11-15, 1862. Battle of Fredericksburg, Va. No 48. Report of Capt. Andrew Cowan, First New York Battery.

[liii] Ibid.

[liv] O.R. Series I, Vol. XXI, Dec. 11-15, 1862. Battle of Fredericksburg, Va. No 48. Report of Capt. Andrew Cowan, First New York Battery.

[lv] Patricia Faust, editor, ***H**istorical Times Illustrated Encyclopedia of the Civil War*, 289-290; Stephen Foster, *The Civil War Cards: The People, The Places, The Politics, The Action: Battle of Fredericksburg*, Atlas Editions, Durham, Connecticut, 1994.

[lvi] Faust, 289-290.

[lvii] O.R. Series I, Vol. XXI, Dec. 11-15, 1862. Battle of Fredericksburg, Va. No 48. Report of Capt. Andrew Cowan, First New York Battery.

[lviii] O.R. Series I, Vol. XXI, No. 47. Report of Capt Gustavus De Russy, 4th U.S. Artillery, commanding batteries on the left.

[lix] Patricia Faust, editor, *Historical Times Illustrated Encyclopedia of the Civil War*, 128; Stephen Foster, *The Civil War Cards: The People, The Places, The Politics, The Action: Battle of Chancellorsville*, Atlas Editions, 1994.

[lx] Ibid.

[lxi] Ibid.

[lxii] Ibid.

[lxiii] Ibid.

[lxiv] O.R. Series I, Vol. XXV/1, April 27-May 6, 1863-The Chancellorsville Campaign. No 266-Report of Brig. Gen. Albion P. Howe, U. S. Army, commanding Second Division.

[lxv] Ibid.

[lxvi] O.R. Series I, Vol. XXVI/1 April 27-May 6, 1863. The Chancellorsville Campaign. No. 232. Report of Capt. Andrew Cowan, First Battery, New York Light Artillery.

[lxvii] O.R. Series I, Vol. XXV/1, April 27-May 6, 1863-The Chancellorsville Campaign. No 266-Report of Brig. Gen. Albion P. Howe, U. S. Army, commanding Second Division.

[lxviii] R.L. Murray, *Hurray for the Ould Flag*, 58.

[lxix] O.R. Series I, Vol. XXVI/1 April 27-May 6, 1863. The Chancellorsville Campaign. No. 232. Report of Capt. Andrew Cowan, First Battery, New York Light Artillery.

[lxx] Patricia Faust, editor, *Historical Times Illustrated Encyclopedia of the Civil War*, 129; Stephen Foster, *The Civil War Cards: The People, The Places, The Politics, The Action: Battle of Fredericksburg*, Atlas Editions, 1994.

[lxxi] Patricia Faust, *Historical Times Encyclopedia of the Civil War*, 307; Stephen Foster, *The Civil War Cards: The People, The Places, The Politics, The Action: Battle of Gettysburg*, Atlas Editions, 1994.

[lxxii] Patricia Faust, *Historical Times Illustrated Encyclopedia of the Civil War*, 308. Stephen Foster, *The Civil War Cards: The People, The Places, The Politics, The Action Battle of Gettysburg*, Atlas Editions, 1994.

[lxxiii] Ibid.

[lxxiv] John Russell Bartlett, *Memoirs of Rhode Island Officers Who Were Engaged In the Service of Their Country During the Great Rebellion of the South*, Sidney S. Rider & Brother, 1867, 373-376.

[lxxv] Col. Andrew Cowan at Gettysburg, *The Louisville Courier Journal*, July 10, 1913.

[lxxvi] Patricia Faust, *The Historical Times Illustrated Encyclopedia of the Civil War*, 305; Stephen Foster, *The Civil War Cards: The People, The Places, The Politics, The Action Battle of Gettysburg*, Atlas Editions, 1994.

[lxxvii] Kent Masterson Brown, "Double Canister at Ten Yards:" Captain Andrew Cowan at Gettysburg, (*The Filson Club History Quarterly*, Vol. 59, No. 3, 1985), 320.

[lxxviii] Andrew Cowan, "When Cowan's Battery Withstood Pickett's Charge," *The Pittsburg Press*, July 2, 1911.

[lxxix] Cowan, "When Cowan's Battery Withstood Pickett's Charge," *The Pittsburg Press*, July 2, 1911.

[lxxx] Cowan, "When Cowan's Battery Withstood Pickett's Charge," *The Pittsburg Press*, July 2, 1911.

[lxxxi] Ibid.

[lxxxii] Ibid.

[lxxxiii] Ibid.

[lxxxiv] Ibid.

[lxxxv] Ibid.

[lxxxvi] Patricia Faust, editor, *The Historical Times Illustrated Encyclopedia of the Civil War*, 307.

[lxxxvii] Cowan, "When Cowan's Battery Withstood Pickett's Charge," *The Pittsburg Press*, July 2, 1911.

[lxxxviii] Ibid.

[lxxxvix] Ibid.

[xc] Ibid.

[xci] Ibid.

[xcii] Ibid.

[xciii] Kent Masterson Brown, "Double Canister at Ten Yards:" Captain Andrew Cowan at Gettysburg, (*The Filson Club History Quarterly*, Vol. 59, No. 3, 1985), 320.

[xciv] Cowan, "When Cowan's Battery Withstood Pickett's Charge," *The Pittsburg Press*, July 2, 1911.

[xcv] Ibid.

[xcvi] Ibid.

[xcvii] Ibid.

[xcviii] Ibid.

[xcix] Kent Masterson Brown, "Double Canister at Ten Yards:" Captain Andrew Cowan at Gettysburg, 321.

[c] Ibid, 322.

[ci] Jeffrey Wert, *Gettysburg: Day Three*, (Simon & Schuster, New York, 2002), 225.

[cii] Cowan, "When Cowan's Battery Withstood Pickett's Charge," *The Pittsburg Press*, July 2, 1911.

[ciii] Ibid.

[civ] Stephen T. Foster, *The Civil War Cards: The People, The Places, The Politics, The Action: Battle of Gettysburg*, Atlas Editions, 1994.

[cv] O.R. Series I, Vol. XXVII/1 [s#43]-Gettysburg Campaign, No. 239, Report of Captain Andrew Cowan, First New York Independent Battery.

[cvi] Cowan, "When Cowan's Battery Withstood Pickett's Charge," *The Pittsburg Press*, July 2, 1911.

[cvii] Ibid.

[cviii] Col. Andrew Cowan at Gettysburg, *The Louisville Courier Journal*, July 10, 1913.

[cix] Ibid.

[cx] Stephen Foster, *Retreat From Gettysburg*, Atlas Editions.

[cxi] Patricia Faust, editor, *The Historical Times Illustrated Encyclopedia of the Civil War*, 307.

[cxii] Tented Gettysburg Swept by Storm, *The Louisville Courier-Journal*, July 3, 1913.

[cxiii] Col. Andrew Cowan at Gettysburg, *The Louisville Courier Journal*, July 10, 1913.

[cxiv] O.R. Series I, Vol. XXVII/1 The Gettysburg Campaign. No 239. Report of Capt. Andrew Cowan, First New York Battery.

[cxv] Stephen Foster, *The Civil War Cards: The People, The Places, The Politics, The Action:* Mine Run Campaign: Botched Union Advance, Atlas Editions, 1994.

[cxvi] O.R. Series I, Vol. XXIX/1 November 26-Decemebr 2, 1863. The Mine Run Campaign near Brandy Station, Virginia. Andrew Cowan, Captain, First Independent Battery, N.Y.S. Vols.

[cxvii] Patricia Faust, *Historical Times Illustrated Encyclopedia of the Civil War*, 497.

[cxviii] R.L. Murray, *Hurrah for the Ould Flag, Captain Andrew Cowan and the First New York Independent Battery at Gettysburg*, (Benedum Books, New York, 1998), Appendix One.

[cxix] Patricia Faust, editor, *The Historical Times Illustrated Encyclopedia of the Civil War*, 551.

[cxx] O.R. Series I, Vol. XXXVI/1 May 4-June 12, 1864. Campaign from the Rapidan to the James River, Va. No 184 Report of Andrew Cowan, First New York Battery.

[cxxi] Stephen T. Foster, *The Civil War Cards: The People, The Places, The Politics, The Action: Battle of the Wilderness*, Atlas Editions, 1994.

[cxxii] Ibid.

[cxxiii] Stephen T. Foster, *The Civil War Cards: The People, The Places, The Politics, The Action: Battle of Spotsylvania*, Atlas Editions, 1994.

[cxxiv] O.R. Series I, Vol. XXXVI/1 May 4-June 12, 1864. Campaign from the Rapidan to the James River, Va. No 184 Report of Andrew Cowan, First New York Battery.

[cxxv] Stephen T. Foster, *The Civil War Cards: The People, The Places, The Politics, The Action: Battles of the Spotsylvania*, Atlas Editions, 1994.

[cxxvi] Stephen T. Foster, *The Civil War Cards: The People, The Places, The Politics, The Action: Battle of Spotsylvania*, Atlas Editions, 1994.

[cxxvii] O.R. Series I, Vol. XXXVI/1 May 4-June 12, 1864. Campaign from the Rapidan to the James River, Va. No 184 Report of Andrew Cowan, First New York Battery.

[cxxviii] Gregory Jaynes, *The Killing Ground: Wilderness to Cold Harbor*, (Time Life Books, Alexandria, Virginia, 1986), 100-105.

[cxxix] O.R. Series I, Vol. XXXVI/1 May 4-June 12, 1864. Campaign from the Rapidan to the James River, Va. No 184 Report of Andrew Cowan, First New York Battery.

[cxxx] Gregory Jaynes, *The Killing Ground: Wilderness to Cold Harbor*, (Time Life Books, Alexandria, Virginia, 1986), 125.

[cxxxi] Stephen T. Foster, *The Civil War Cards: The People, The Places, The Politics, The Action:* Battle of Harris Farm, Atlas Editions, 1994; Gregory Jaynes, *The Killing Ground: Wilderness to Cold Harbor*, (Time Life Books, Alexandria, Virginia, 1986), 125-126.

[cxxxii] Stephen T. Foster, *The Civil War Cards: The People, The Places, The Politics, The Action: North Anna Campaign: The Trap is Set*, Atlas Editions, 1994; Gregory Jaynes, *The Killing Ground: Wilderness to Cold Harbor*, (Time Life Books, Alexandria, Virginia, 1986), 130-131.

[cxxxiii] Stephen T. Foster, *The Civil War Cards: The People, The Places, The Politics, The Action: North Anna Campaign: Earthworks Too Formidable*, Atlas Editions, 1994; Gregory Jaynes, *The Killing Ground: Wilderness to Cold Harbor*, (Time Life Books, Alexandria, Virginia, 1986), 131-134.

[cxxxiv] Gregory Jaynes, *The Killing Ground: Wilderness to Cold Harbor*, (Time Life Books, Alexandria, Virginia, 1986), 134-136.

[cxxxv] Stephen T. Foster, *The Civil War Cards: The People, The Places, The Politics, The Action:* Battle of Cold Harbor: Stalemate, Atlas Editions, 1994.; Gregory Jaynes, *The Killing Ground: Wilderness to Cold Harbor*, (Time Life Books, Alexandria, Virginia, 1986), 152-153.

[cxxxvi] O.R. Series I, Vol. XXXVI/1 May 4-June 12, 1864. Campaign from the Rapidan to the James River, Va. No 184 Report of Andrew Cowan, First New York Battery.

[cxxxvii] Stephen Foster, *The Civil War Cards: The People, The Places, The Politics, The Action: Battle of Cold Harbor: Stalemate*, Atlas Editions, 1994.

[cxxxviii] Stephen T. Foster, *The Civil War Cards: The People, The Places, The Politics, The Action: The Battle of Cold Harbor: Not War But Murder, Volley of Hurtling Death*, Atlas Editions, 1994.

[cxxxix] O.R. Series I, Vol. XXXVI/1 May 4-June 12, 1864. Campaign from the Rapidan to the James River, Va. No 184 Report of Andrew Cowan, First New York Battery.

[cxl] Gregory Jaynes, *The Killing Ground: Wilderness to Cold Harbor*, (Time Life Books, Alexandria, Virginia, 1986), 169.

[cxli] O.R. Series I, Vol. XL/1 June 13-July 31, 1864. The Richmond, Va. Campaign. No 170 Report of Capt. Andrew Cowan, First New York Battery , of operations June 13-July 12.

[cxlii] Glorify His Name: All Elements Unite in Service to His Memory, The Louisville Courier-Journal, Feb. 13, 1909.

[cxliii] Patricia Faust, editor, *Historical Times Illustrated Encyclopedia of the Civil War*, 279.

[cxliv] O.R. Series I, Vol. XXXVII/1 [#70] June 23-August 8, 1864-Operations in the Shenandoah Valley, Maryland, and Pennsylvania. No. 48. Report of Captain Andrew Cowan, First New York Battery, of operations July 11-30.

[cxlv] O.R. Series I, Vol. XXXVII/1 [#70] June 23-August 8, 1864-Operations in the Shenandoah Valley, Maryland, and Pennsylvania. No. 48. Report of Captain Andrew Cowan, First New York Battery, of operations July 11-30.

[cxlvi] Patricia Faust, editor, *Historical Times Illustrated Encyclopedia of the Civil War*, 678.

[cxlvii] Patricia Faust, Ibid.

[cxlviii] O.R. Series I, Vol. XLIII/1 [#90] August 7-November 28, 1864-The Shenandoah Valley Campaign. No. 11-Reports of Maj. Gen. Horatio Wright, U.S. Army, commanding Sixth Army Corps, of operations August 6-October 10 and October 19.

[cxlix] Patricia Faust, *Historical Times Illustrated Encyclopedia of the Civil War*, 678.

[cl] O.R. Series I, Vol. XLIII/1 [#90] August 7-November 28, 1864-The Shenandoah Valley Campaign. No. 75 Reports of Lieutenant Orsamus R. Van Etten, First New York Battery, of operations September 19-October 19.

[cli] Ibid.

[clii] Ibid.

[cliii] Ibid.

[cliv] Ibid.

[clv] Patricia Faust, *Historical Times Illustrated Encyclopedia of the Civil War*, 678-679.

[clvi] Glorify Name of Lincoln: All Elements Unite in Service to his Memory, *The Louisville Courier-Journal*, Feb. 13, 1909.

[clvii] Korn, Jerry, *Pursuit to Appomattox: The Last Battles*, Time Life Books, Richmond, Virginia, 1987, 92-93.

[clviii] Korn, Jerry, *Pursuit to Appomattox: The Last Battles*, Time Life Books, Richmond, Virginia, 1987, 78-79.

[clix] Korn, *Pursuit to Appomattox: The Last Battles*, 79-81.

[clx] Korn, 81-90.

[clxi] Korn, 91-92.

[clxii] O.R. Series I, Vol. XLVI/1. March 29-April 9, 1865. The Appomattox Campaign. No 147. Report of Captain Andrew Cowan, First Battery New York Light Artillery, commanding Artillery Brigade.

[clxiii] O.R. Series I, Vol. XLVI/1. March 29-April 9, 1865. The Appomattox Campaign. No 147. Report of Captain Andrew Cowan, First Battery New York Light Artillery, commanding Artillery Brigade.

[clxiv] O.R. Series I, Vol. XLVI/1. March 29-April 9, 1865. The Appomattox Campaign. No 147. Report of Captain Andrew Cowan, First Battery New York Light Artillery, commanding Artillery Brigade.

[clxv] O.R. Series I, Vol. XLVI/1. March 29-April 9, 1865. The Appomattox Campaign. No 147. Report of Captain Andrew Cowan, First Battery New York Light Artillery, commanding Artillery Brigade.

[clxvi] Korn, Jerry, *Pursuit to Appomattox: The Last Battles*, 92-93.

[clxvii] Korn, 97.

[clxviii] Korn, 110.

[clxix] O.R. Series I, Vol. XLVI/1. March 29-April 9, 1865. The Appomattox Campaign. No 147. Report of Captain Andrew Cowan, First Battery New York Light Artillery, commanding Artillery Brigade.

[clxx] O.R. Series I, Vol. XLVI/1. March 29-April 9, 1865. The Appomattox Campaign. No 147. Report of Captain Andrew Cowan, First Battery New York Light Artillery, commanding Artillery Brigade.

[clxxi] Korn, 152.

[clxxii] Glorify Name of Lincoln: All Elements Unite in Service to his Memory, *The Louisville Courier-Journal*, Feb. 13, 1909.

[clxxiii] O.R. Series I, Vol. XLVI/3 [#97] Union Correspondence, Orders, and Returns relating to operations in Northern and southeastern

Virginia, West Virginia, Maryland, and Pennsylvania, from March 16, 1865 to June 30, 1865. General Orders No. 19.

[clxxiv] Great Tribute Paid Col. Andrew Cowan by National Tribune, *The Louisville Courier- Journal*, August 4, 1912.

[clxxv] Ibid.

[clxxvi] Ibid.

[clxxvii] Bryan Bush, *Louisville's Southern Exposition: 1883-1887; The City of Progress*, (The History Press, Charleston, 2011), 21.

[clxxviii] The Southern Exposition, *The Kentucky Explorer*, June 1996, 38-39.

[clxxix] Bryan Bush, *Louisville's Southern Exposition*, 22.

[clxxx] *The Louisville Courier-Journal*, August 2, 1883, 11.

[clxxxi] Ibid.

[clxxxii] Bryan Bush, *Louisville's Southern Exposition*, 25-28.

[clxxxiii] Bryan Bush, *Louisville's Southern Exposition*, 33.

[clxxxiv] Bryan Bush, *Louisville's Southern Exposition*, 44-45.

[clxxxv] Bryan Bush, *Louisville's Southern Exposition*, 50.

[clxxxvi] Andrew Cowan, The Day After: A Walk Through the Exposition Building Yesterday…., *The Louisville Courier-Journal*, Nov. 12, 1883.

[clxxxvii] Andrew Cowan, The Day After: A Walk Through the Exposition Building Yesterday…., *The Louisville Courier-Journal*, Nov. 12, 1883.

[clxxxviii] Ibid.

[clxxxix] Ibid.

[cxc] Ibid.

[cxci] Bryan Bush, *Louisville's Southern Exposition*, 51-52.

[cxcii] Ibid, 59.

[cxciii] Ibid, 71.

[cxciv] The Art Gallery of the Polytechnic Society opened last night by President Young, *The Louisville Courier-Journal*, May 21, 1884.

[cxcv] George Yater, *Two Hundred Years at the Falls of the Ohio: A History of Louisville and Jefferson County*, (The Heritage Corporation, Louisville, Kentucky, 1979), 122-123.

[cxcvi] http://www.statueofliberty.org/statue_history.html

[cxcvii] Ibid.

[cxcviii] http://www.history.com/topics/statue-of-liberty

[cxcix] Ibid.

[cc] The *Louisville Courier-Journal*, The Statue of Liberty: A Subscription from Kentuckians Asked For, November 30, 1883.

[cci] Ibid.

[ccii] E. Polk Johnston, *A History of Kentucky and Kentuckians: The Leaders, Representative Men in Commerce, Industry, and Modern Activities*, Vol. II, 1912, 1024-1026.

[cciii] Louisville's parks vision set forth 125 years ago, Steve Wiser, *The Louisville Courier-Journal*, June 3, 2012.

[cciv] Andrew Cowan, City Politics: Col Andrew Cowan Accepts the Call as a Non-political Park Commissioner, *The Louisville Courier-Journal*, September 27, 1893.

[ccv] Louisville's parks vision set forth 125 years ago, Steve Wiser, *The Louisville Courier-Journal*, June 3, 2012.

[ccvi] Ibid.

[ccvii] Patricia Dalton Haragon, *The Olmstead Parks of Louisville, A Botanical Field Guide*, (Lexington, University Press of Kentucky, 2014), 2-3.

[ccviii] Andrew Cowan, City Politics: Col Andrew Cowan Accepts the Call as a Non-political Park Commissioner, *The Louisville Courier-Journal*, September 27, 1893.

[ccix] Ibid.

[ccx] Col. Cowan Chosen Against His Will, *The Louisville Courier-Journal*, Nov 28, 1894.

[ccxi] E. Polk Johnston, *A History of Kentucky and Kentuckians: The Leaders, Representative Men in Commerce, Industry, and Modern Activities*, Vol. II, 1912, 1024-1026.

[ccxii] John Kleber, editor, *The Encyclopedia of Louisville, The University Press of Kentucky*, 2001, 690.

[ccxiii] Ibid, 691.

[ccxiv] The Grand Army at Gettysburg, *The New York Times*, July 4, 1886.

[ccxv] *On the Battlefield Again: The Blue and the Gray at Gettysburg, The New York Times*, July 4, 1887.

[ccxvi] Ibid.

[ccxvii] Ibid.

[ccxviii] Ibid.

[ccxix] *On the Battlefield Again: The Blue and the Gray at Gettysburg, The New York Times*, July 4, 1887.

[ccxx] Accidental Explosion Kills Five From Louisville Legion, The Kentucky National Guard History eMuseum, www.kynghistory.ky.gov/history

[ccxxi] William Cummings, Pomp, Pandemonium, and Paramours: The G. A. R. Convention of 1895, *The Register of the Kentucky Historical Society*, Vol. 81, No. 3, 1983, 274.

[ccxxii] Grand Army Encampment; Veterans Received with Great Honors in Louisville, *Louisville Courier-Journal,* September 10, 1895.

[ccxxiii] William Cummings, Pomp, Pandemonium, and Paramours: The G. A. R. Convention of 1895, *The Register of the Kentucky Historical Society*, Vol. 81, No. 3, 1983, 277.

[ccxxiv] Ibid, 278.

[ccxxv] William Cummings, Pomp, Pandemonium, and Paramours: The G. A. R. Convention of 1895, The Register of the Kentucky Historical Society, Vol. 81, No. 3, 1983, 281.; Accidental Explosion Kills Five From Louisville Legion, The Kentucky National Guard History eMuseum, www.kynghistory.ky.gov/history

[ccxxvi] Accidental Explosion Kills Five From Louisville Legion, The Kentucky National Guard History eMuseum, www.kynghistory.ky.gov/history.

[ccxxvii] William Cummings, Pomp, Pandemonium, and Paramours: The G. A. R. Convention of 1895, *The Register of the Kentucky Historical Society*, Vol. 81, No. 3, 1983, 283.

[ccxxviii] Ibid, 283.

[ccxxix] Touching Incident: Greeting Between Col. Cowan and his Old Comrades, *The Louisville Courier Journal*, September 9, 1895.

[ccxxx] A Tree of Peace: Yew Oak from Pennsylvania Planted In Eastern Park, Col. Castleman and Col. Cowan Formally Declare that the War is Over., *The Louisville Courier-Journal*, September 11, 1895.

[ccxxxi] Ibid.

[ccxxxii] Praises: Of the City From Gen. Lawler, Afternoon at the Galt House, Thinks this will be the most successful Encampment that has been held, He and other Prominent Persons dine with Col. Cowan, *The Louisville Courier-Journal*, September 10, 1895.

[ccxxxiii] Strong Ties: Bind the Blue and Gray National Park, Captain John Leathers and Col. Andrew Cowan Speak, *The Louisville Courier-Journal*, September 12, 1895.

[ccxxxiv] All Pleased: Feeling of the Citizens G.A.R. Committee: Everything Went Well. *The Louisville Courier-Journal*, September 15, 1895.

[ccxxxv] Mrs. Pickett Wears the Blue, *The Louisville Courier-Journal*, June 2, 1900.

[ccxxxvi] Ibid.

[ccxxxvii] Men In Gray Show Their Love for One in Blue, Loving Cup for Col. Cowan, *The Louisville Courier Journal*, June 28, 1905.

[ccxxxviii] Ibid.

[ccxxxix] Ibid.

[ccxl] Ibid.

[ccxli] Ibid.

[ccxlii] Col. Andrew Cowan in Confederate Gray, *The Louisville Courier-Journal*, June 14, 1905.

[ccxliii] The Abraham Lincoln Birthplace, The National Park Service.

[ccxliv] Put In Charge: General Williams Marshal at Lincoln Celebration, *The Louisville Courier-Journal*, Feb. 9, 1909.

[ccxlv] Ibid.

[ccxlvi] Glorify Name of Lincoln: All Elements Unite in Service to his Memory, *The Louisville-Courier Journal*, Feb. 13, 1909.

[ccxlvii] Ibid.

[ccxlviii] Ibid.

[ccxlix] Ibid.

[ccl] Four Local Gettysburg Survivors to Attend Fiftieth Anniversary, *The Louisville Courier-Journal*, Jan. 29, 1912.

[ccli] Kentuckians Assist Gettysburg Commission, The Louisville Courier-Journal, May 29, 1913.

[cclii] Blue and Gray Reunion Ends, *The Louisville Courier-Journal*, July 6, 1913.

[ccliii] Ibid.

[ccliv] Ibid.

[cclv] Ibid.

[cclvi] Ibid.

[cclvii] Ibid.

[cclviii] Gettysburg Peace Memorial, *The Louisville Courier-Journal*, Sept. 23, 1913.

[cclix] For Memorial at Gettysburg, Col. Andrew Cowan Successfully Organizes Association, *The Louisville Courier Journal*, Sept. 20, 1913.

cclx Ibid.

cclxi Col. Cowan Again Honored by Comrades in Arms, The Louisville Courier-Journal, October 4, 1913.

cclxii Mr. Taft Attends Loyal Legion Banquet, *The Louisville Courier-Journal*, May 7, 1914.

cclxiii A Breezy Speech: All About the Boys that Wore the Blue, *The Louisville Courier-Journal*, May 13, 1914.

cclxiv Ibid.

cclxv Confederate Hosts To Take Washington, Veterans of the Gray Invited to Hold Annual Reunion at the Capital, *The New York Times*, Oct. 4, 1915.

cclxvi Ibid.

cclxvii Col. Cowan Showered with Praise on U.C.V. Reunion Plan, *The Louisville Courier-Journal*, November 12, 1915.

cclxviii Webb Statue Unveiled, Union General Honored at "Bloody Angle" on Gettysburg Field, *The New York Times*, October 13, 1915.

cclxix Col. Cowan Expresses Hope All Kentucky Will Revere Lincoln, *The Louisville Courier-Journal*, April 14, 1915.

cclxx Ibid.

cclxxi Ibid.

cclxxii Ibid.

cclxxiii Ibid.

cclxxiv Wilson Pledges Nation's All In War, The New York Times, June 6, 1917.

cclxxv Ibid.

cclxxvi Ibid.

cclxxvii Cowan Funeral Set For Today, *The Louisville Courier-Journal*, August 24, 1919; Col. Andrew Cowan Dead, Father of the Joint Reunion of Blue and Gray at Gettysburg, *The New York Times*, August 24, 1919.

cclxxviii Cowan Funeral Set For Today, *The Louisville Courier-Journal*, August 24, 1919.

cclxxix Col. Cowan Was Leader In Many Louisville Activities, *The Louisville Courier-Journal*, August 24, 1919.

cclxxx Col. Cowan Is Laid to Rest, *The Louisville-Courier Journal*, August 25, 1919.

cclxxxi Cowan Estate Worth $450,000. Bulk to be Held in Trust For Benefit of his Widow, *The Louisville Courier-Journal*, August 29, 1919.

[cclxxxii] Memorials in Park Planned, *The Louisville Courier-Journal*, November 18, 1919.

[cclxxxiii] Accessory Business of Cowan Company Large, *The Louisville Courier Journal*, March 16, 1921.

References

Books

Bailey, Ronald, *Forward to Richmond: McClellan's Peninsular Campaign*, Time Life Books, Alexandria, Virginia, 1983.

Bailey, Ronald, *The Bloodiest Day: The Battle of Antietam*, Times Life Books, Alexandria, Virginia, 1984.

Bartlett, John R., *Memoirs of Rhode Island Officers and the Officers who were engaged in the service of the their county during the Great Rebellion of the South*, Sidney S. Rider & Brother, 1867.

Bush, Bryan, *Louisville's Southern Exposition: 1883-1887: The City of Progress*, The History Press, 2011.

Davis, William C., *The Battlefields of the Civil War*, Salamander Books, New York, 1991.

Faust, Patricia, editor, *Historical Times Illustrated Encyclopedia of the Civil War*, New York, Harper & Row, 1986.

Gottfried, Bradley, *The Artillery of Gettysburg*, Cumberland House Publishing, Inc., Nashville, Tennessee, 2008.

Goolrick, William, *Rebels Resurgent: Fredericksburg to Chancellorsville*, Time Life Books, Alexandria, Virginia, 1985.

Kleber, John, *The Encyclopedia of Louisville*, Lexington, The University of Kentucky Press, 2001.

Korn, Jerry, *Pursuit to Appomattox: The Last Battles*, Time Life Books, Alexandria, Virginia, 1987.

Jayes, Gregory, *The Killing Ground: Wilderness to Cold Harbor*, Time Life Books, Alexandria, Virginia, 1986.

Johnston, E. Polk, *A History of Kentucky and Kentuckians: The Leaders, Representative Men in Commerce, Industry, and Modern Activities*, Volume II, Lewis Publishing Company, Chicago & New York, 1912.

Murray, R.L., *Hurrah for the Ould Flag!: Captain Andrew Cowan and the First New York Independent Battery at Gettysburg*, Benedum Books, New York, 1998.

Pierro, Joseph, *The Maryland Campaign of September 1862: Ezra A. Carman's Definitive Study of the Union and Confederate Armies at Antietam*, Routledge, New York, 2008.

Sears, Stephen, *Chancellorsville*, Houghton Mifflin Company, New York, 1996.

Sears, Stephen, *To The Gates of Richmond: The Peninsular Campaign*, Houghton Mifflin Books, 1992.

Sears, Stephen, *Landscape Turned Red: The Battle of Antietam*, Ticknor & Fields, 1983.

Wert, Jeffrey, *Gettysburg: Day Three*, New York, Simon & Schuster, 2001.

Other Resources

Foster, Stephen, *The Civil War Cards: The People, The Places, The Politics, The Action*, Atlas Editions, Durham, Connecticut, 1994.

The War of the Rebellion: a Compilation of the Official Records of the Union and Confederate Armies, Government Printing Office, Washington, D.C., 1880-1901.

Articles

Brown, Kent Masterson, "Double Canister at Ten Yards:" Captain Andrew Cowan at Gettysburg, Vol. 59, No. 3, *The Filson Club History Quarterly*, 1985, 293-326.

Cummings, William, Pomp, Pandemonium, and Paramours; The G.A.R. Convention of 1895, *The Register of the Kentucky Historical Society*, 81, No. 3, 1983, 274-286.

Wiser, Steven, Before Olmstead: Inspiration Behind the Louisville Parks System, Louisville Historical League

Accidental Explosion Kills Five From Louisville Legion, The Kentucky National Guard History eMuseum.

Newspapers

The Louisville Courier-Journal

The Pittsburg Press

The New York Times

About the Author

Bryan Bush was born in 1966 in Louisville, Kentucky and has been a native of that city ever since. He graduated with honors from Murray State University with a degree in History and Psychology, and received his Master's Degree from the University of Louisville in 2005.

Bryan has always had a passion for history, especially the Civil War. He has been a member of many different Civil War historical preservation societies, has consulted for movie companies and other authors, coordinated with other museums on displays of various museum articles and artifacts, has written for magazines, such as *Kentucky Civil War Magazine*, *North/South Trader*, *The Kentucky Civil War Bugle* and *Back Home in Kentucky* and worked for many different historical sites, and has always fought hard to maintain and preserve Civil War history in the Western Theater. In 1999, Bryan published his first work: *The Civil War Battles of the Western Theater*. Since then, Mr. Bush has had published over thirteen books on the Civil War including *Lloyd Tilghman: Confederate General in the Western Theater; Louisville During the Civil War: A History and*

Guide; Lincoln and the Speeds: An Enduring and Devoted Friendship; Butcher Burbridge: Union General Stephen Gano Burbridge and his Reign of Terror over Kentucky; Louisville's Southern Exposition: The City of Progress, and *Haunted Battlefields of the South, Resting in Peace: Civil War Leaders In Cave Hill Cemetery.*

Bryan Bush has been a Civil War re-enactor for fourteen years, portraying an artillerist. For five years Bryan was on the Board of Directors and curator for the Old Bardstown Civil War Museum and Village: The Battles of the Western Theater Museum in Bardstown, Kentucky and is currently a board member for the Louisville Historical League and is the official Civil War tour guide for Cave Hill Cemetery.

Index

C

D

E

F

G

H

I

J

K

L

M

Y

Z

Other Acclaim Press Books by Bryan Bush

Lloyd Tilghman
Confederate General in the Western Theatre

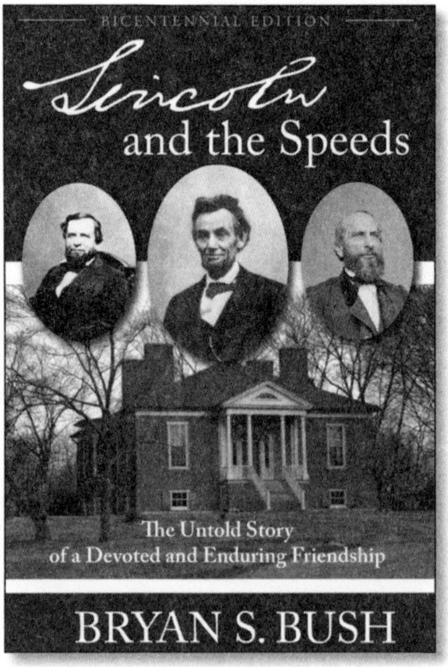

Lincoln and the Speeds
The Untold Story of a Devoted and Enduring Friendship

Butcher Burbridge
Union General Stephen Burbridge and His Reign of Terror Over Kentucky